Where Angels Deserve to Die

ATF – Rogue Agents or Rogue Agency? A Former Agent's History

Adam K. Ging

ISBN Number 978-0-9839813-0-5

Library of Congress Control Number: 2011916124

Disclaimer: Everything you are about to read is true. All of it. All names have been changed to protect the innocent. Oh, and the *not* so innocent. Moreover, this is not a law enforcement training manual; therefore, the author and publisher disclaim any liability incurred in connection with anything discussed or elaborated upon in this book, nor suggest or condone any methods used herein.

Printed in the United States of America

A publication of Chaos AG Publications, LLC

For my father, who made me who I am,

For my son, who made me proud of who I am,

For my angelic sister Anna, who says a prayer for me every day,

And for that brown haired/brown eyed girl across the bar,
who changed my life forever.

And I raise my head and stare
Into the eyes of a stranger
I've always known that the mirror never lies

QUEENSRŸCHE

If I know I'm going crazy, I must not be insane.

Dave Mustaine/David Ellefson

Contents

Part Three: Valley of the Sun

Part Four: The Future (?)

Author's Note

There is both pain and pleasure that permeate these pages. There are things of which I am extremely proud, things that I regret, as well as incidents that are downright shameful. Not all pertain to your humble narrator. If the passages that follow be a prose-written confession, then so be it because it is the truth.

These pages also do not glorify myself or ATF; they are merely an inside look at an agent's career and the duplicity he witnessed and/or experienced firsthand at the hands of his employer – some warranted, though mostly not. Contrary to popular belief, being a federal investigator isn't being James Bond. Moreover, the Bureau of Alcohol, Tobacco, Firearms and Explosives isn't the CIA or MI6. It is a federal agency currently circling the drain and grasping at straws to maintain its very existence. This will be detailed at length.

Many names in the book have been changed – as noted by asterisk*. This was mostly done to protect innocent and blameless people. In regards to street gangs, names were changed to preclude them from receiving any notoriety or *infamy*, as they would like to say. I refuse/resist to glorify any gang name, area, or pathetic affiliation – though I will use the terms Crip, Blood, and others on many occasions. My only point here is that I have not, nor will I ever glorify a street gang member or his band of "outlaws." To me they are weak and useless human beings that don't merit any formal recognition. Some may have cast a shadow, but rest assured it was always fleeting.

Yet, as one reads these pages, he'll see an opacity develop that blurs the demarcation of good and bad, of what's necessary and of what also cannot be avoided. To that this book is dedicated.

Here's something you won't normally find in an Author's Notes, but it's a good way to get to know who I am before you begin your journey through these pages:

<u>Favorite Bands</u>:
Metallica & Tool

Favorite Books:

East of Eden	*Great Expectations*
The Bible	*The Rise and Fall of the Third Reich*
Dark Sun	*The Plutonium Files*
Of Mice and Men	*Oliver Twist*
Plato's The Republic	*L'Emile*
The Disappearing Spoon	*The Pillars of the Earth*
Cadillac Desert	*Two Years Before the Mast*
The Prince	*The Godfather*

Favorite Songs:

"Simple Man" - Lynyrd Skynyrd

"Comfortably Numb" - Pink Floyd

"Twenty-Nine Palms" , "Confrontation" - Tangerine Dream

"Fade to Black", "One" - Metallica

"Right in Two" , "Stinkfist", "Ticks and Leeches"-Tool

"Listen to Your Heart","Fading Like a Flower"-Roxette

"Let it Be"-The Beatles

"I'd Love to Change the World" - Ten Years After

"Astronomy", "Don't Fear the Reaper" "Last Days of May" - Blue Öyster Cult

"Everlong" - Foo Fighters

"Promises in the Dark", "Hell is for Children", "Precious Time" - Pat Benatar

"Á Tout le Monde" - Megadeth

"Hallowed Be Thy Name", "The Trooper" - Iron Maiden

"Just What I Needed" - The Cars

"I Got a Name" - Jim Croce

"It's Alright", "Heaven and Hell" - Black Sabbath

"Fight the Good Fight" - Triumph

"Raining Blood" - Slayer

"Featherwood" - RK & AKG

"Live to Tell" - Madonna

"Love to Love" - UFO

"No Quarter" - Led Zeppelin

"Empire", "I Don't Believe in Love" - Queensryche

"Imagine" - John Lennon

"I Am the Law" - Anthrax

"A Nation on Fire" - Machine Head

"Sounds of Silence" - Simon and Garfunkel

"Eve of Destruction" - Barry Maguire
"Would?" Alice in Chains
"Cowboy Song", "Renegade" - Thin Lizzy
"Because the Night" - Patty Smith
"Cats in the Cradle" - Harry Chapin
"Green Grass and High Tides" – Outlaws
"Dream On" - Aerosmith

Hollywood's Top Shelf/Favorite Role:

Clint Eastwood	Dirty Harry
[And there's a reason he's placed at the Top]	
Paul Newman	Butch Cassidy
Henry Fonda	Frank
Jimmy Stewart	George Bailey
Meryl Streep	Linda
Gene Wilder	Waco Kid
Anthony Quinn	Auda
David Lean	
Don Siegel	
Ted Post	
William Friedkin	
Sidney Lumet	
Leo Penn (and all those blacklisted)	
Martin Scorsese	
John Milius	
Sergio Leone	
Steven Spielberg	
George Lucas	
Francis Coppola	
Al Pacino	Michael
Blake Edwards	
Jack Lemmon	Professor Fate
Groucho Marx	Professor Wagstaff
Harpo Marx	Yourself, w/ Lucille on *I Love Lucy*
Chico Marx	Chico
Lucille Ball	Yourself, w/ Harpo on *I Love Lucy*
Michael Mann	
Robert DeNiro	Max Cady
Johnny Depp	Jack Sparrow
James Caan	Santino

Peter Sellers	Dr. Strangelove
Lloyd Bridges	Samuel Hamilton
Natalie Portman	Mathilda
Gene Hackman	Popeye
Elizabeth Taylor	Martha
My father	Morgan Allen
James Cagney	Cody Jarrett
Humphrey Bogart	Rick
Edward G. Robinson	Little Caesar
Albert Popwell	Mustapha

Favorite Albums:

The Wall – Pink Floyd
Number of the Beast – Iron Maiden
Suffer - Bad Religion
Master of Puppets - Metallica
Reign in Blood - Slayer
Aenima - Tool
Precious Time - Pat Benatar
The Cars - The Cars
Moving Pictures - Rush
Making Movies - Dire Straits
Hardcore 81 - DOA
Never Mind the Bollocks - Sex Pistols
Vulgar Display of Power - Pantera
Boston - Boston
Use Your Illusion - Guns n Roses
Women and Children First - Van Halen
Operation Mindcrime - Queensryche
Rocks - Aerosmith
Running on Empty - Jackson Browne
Live Rust - Neil Young
One for the Road - The Kinks
Shout at the Devil - Motley Crüe
Pyromania - Def Leppard
Roots - Sepultura
Live at Budokan - Cheap Trick
Live Killers - Queen
Back in Black - AC/DC
Burn My Eyes - Machine Head
London Calling - The Clash

Favorite Movies:

Apocalypse Now   *Big Wednesday*
A Fistful of Dollars   *White Heat*
For a Few Dollars More   *Heat*
The Good, the Bad, and the Ugly *Ben Hur*
The Great Race   *Gojira*
American History X   *Summer of '42*
Dr. Strangelove   *Animal House*
The Front Page   *Thief*
American Graffiti   *Casablanca*
Bull Durham   *Bananas*
Caddyshack   *Godfather I & II*
Dirty Harry   *Magnum Force*
Lawrence of Arabia   *Angels With Dirty Faces*
Once Upon a Time in the West *High Plains Drifter*
The Roaring Twenties   *Fast Times at Ridgemont High*
Trinity & Beyond – Atomic Bomb Movie
Star Wars   *Smokey and the Bandit*
Blazing Saddles   *The Blues Brothers*
The French Connection   *Deliverance*

Favorite TV Shows:

NFL football   National news
Warner Brothers cartoons   Popeye (black and white)
Get Smart   Gumby

Favorite Role Models/Athletes:

Drew Brees   Shaquille O'Neal
Mark Brunell   Rafael Nadal
Troy Polamalu   Roger Federer
Aaron Rodgers   Steve Yzerman
Tom Brady   Brooks Robinson
Steve Nash   Tony Gwynn
Tim Duncan   Jack Nicklaus
Johnny Miller   Jerry Rice

Favorite Places:

Central California   Maui
France   Joshua Tree National Park
Colorado Rockies   Mt. St. Helens
Pacific Ocean   Pacific Palisades Bluffs

Favorite Foods:
- Steak (filet)
- Seafood
- Fried Chicken
- Italian
- Mexican

Favorite Cars:
- Ford Mustang
- Toyota trucks

Favorite Musical Instrument:
- Electric Guitar – Gibson SG

Favorite Flora:
- Oak trees
- Saguaro Cactus

Favorite Fauna:
- Whales
- Sea Otters
- Tarantulas
- Praying Mantis
- California Sea Lions
- Owls
- Pelicans
- Hummingbirds
- Domestic Cats (those that are homeless – Long Live the Ghetto Kitties!)

Favorite Pastimes:
- Reading
- Writing
- Outdoor activities
- Hanging out with friends
- Doing nothing

Where Angels Deserve to Die

Prologue: Why ATF?

I was born into an interesting household. My father, an ex-Marine, had made his fortune in California as an actor after he and his family had left the dustbowls of Oklahoma during the Great Depression. Many of his relatives had passed from time and memory like many of the Joads in *The Grapes of Wrath*, but my father never lost hope of his vision of being successful in the real world. As a result I grew up in a family that never had to worry about its next meal, though the blue collar ethos was never jettisoned from our daily lives. It became an inculcated trait that I carry to this day.

My father's dream was for his only son to receive a great education. I was a lucky child in that I was blessed with being a good athlete as well as having an intellect that desired to be tested, and my father knew this. As a result he was able to send me to one of the top private high schools in Los Angeles, if not the entire country. I would receive top academic training as well as lettering in football and baseball. At the time I think 98 per cent of all the school's graduates attended college after graduation, something the local high school could not aspire to.

My father knew I would get a good education wherever I went, but he knew I had to be tested. His choice of the private high school proved to be the best money he ever spent on his son. I recite that fact to him to this day. However, there were two drawbacks to this "gift": first, the school was twenty-five miles from my home – thank God for cars; and second, the school sat in downtown Los Angeles, skyscrapers of which stood as sentinels only 1½ to 2 miles away.

My education, I would soon find out, would involve more than books behind the school's walls. I would also learn about life of the inner city. I would quickly learn about drive-by shootings, graffiti, muggings, and all good things associated with inner city life.

Though I was a good student, I was a prankster, an example of which figures into my hiring as a federal agent. At my high school it was the "duty" of the graduating class to perform a prank during its senior year. I'm not sure if any prank was done by other graduates that year (1982), but I came up with one for the ages. A dance was scheduled in the spring of 1982. My idea was to stage a fake punk rock show for the same night and at the very same venue, that is, at the banquet hall of my high school. I had a good friend who was a great artist, and he drew up a fake flyer advertising a punk rock gig for that very same night; the "concert" was to feature five or six of the best LA bands of that era.

I had another friend who worked at a printing shop. Once the flyer/handbill was completed, she printed up 1000 copies for my friends and I to post all over the metropolitan Los Angeles area. We covered three counties, dozens of high schools, known punk rock hangouts and venues, everywhere.

The night of the dance, the street in front of my high school was littered with hundreds, if not thousands, of punk rockers looking to get into the show. Since no punk rock show existed, LAPD had to be called in to take care of the irate crowd. The scene nearly turned into a riot.

Several friends of mine and I arrived at the school after the dance had started. I turned my car into the school but was immediately flagged down and stopped by the assistant principal Ben Bratkowski*. If you've ever seen *Animal House*, well, this clown was Douglas Niedermeyer. As soon as I stopped my car, Bratkowski grabbed me and threw me out of the car; he then ordered everyone else in the vehicle to exit as he began searching. During this questionable Fourth Amendment violation, he recovered a single beer from under the passenger seat. I remember it well – it was a Carlsberg Elephant Malt Liquor bottle, full and unopened. I didn't usually drink this brand, and it had probably been in my car for months. Bratkowski didn't care. He thought he had me for illegal possession of alcohol on campus. Ironically, he also found a stack of flyers that we had failed to post, but since it was dark Bratkowski didn't see what he had. Had he known what those pieces of paper were, I would have been screwed.

I was quickly escorted into the dean's office and told to answer for my crime of illegal alcohol possession. The dean at the time happened to be my defensive backs coach on the football team, and he was a friend. Bratkowski had also been a football coach, but somewhere along the line he had flipped out. I guess the administrative duties went to his head. The dean handed me a piece of paper (one of the flyers) and asked me if I had seen one and if I knew anything about it. I answered "yes" to the former but "no" to the latter. The dean was cool and only told me that I couldn't go to the dance. I, of course, couldn't wait to get the hell out of there, so I accepted the "punishment" gracefully.

I relate this story because during my background investigation prior to being hired in 1990, ATF agents had gone to my high school to interview people, and it just so happened that Bratkowski was the one interviewed. All he could do was proceed to motherfuck the hell out of me to the agents thinking that he could sink my chances of being hired. His strategy backfired. I was told later by the investigating agents that they thought Bratkowski was such an unprofessional asshole that anything he said was taken as pure hogwash. They also told me that after talking to him, they felt that I actually sounded like someone who would be a good, if not great agent. (Thanks for the recommendation Ben; you were pivotal in getting me hired!)

Getting back to my introduction, my high school was surrounded on all sides by gang members, drug runners, the homeless, and somewhat ironically, a huge cemetery on the south. This "turf" was also controlled by a street gang, the Graveyard Boyz. More on them later.

The northern side of the campus became the hotspot for debauchery and criminality. Our chemistry labs were located there, and it became a weekend occurrence for the windows to be shot out. No one was ever hurt, thank God. Also, those outer walls became the local bulletin board for spray-paint graffiti. I'll give the school officials credit, they never let the tagging stay for more than twenty-four hours, but that was only a temporary coup. The writing always returned.

One night during my junior year a friend and I were held up by a couple of Crips as we were drinking beer near the campus. I should have known something was coming, but I blew it off. The two pistol-packing gangbangers, on the other hand, had other things in mind. We were ordered to lay on the ground, and with a gun to my head I quickly learned what fear was and how it affected a poor high school kid being robbed of only five dollars. That's all I had in my wallet.

But I also learned another valuable lesson that night – one that would come into play many years later during my ATF career – I also learned about staring down the barrel of a gun into the eyes of a would-be murderer and knowing *that I was not going to be killed*. I knew I was "safe;" these guys were kids like me and had yet to make the jump from petty criminals to full-fledged maniacal killers.

This extemporaneous education far overshadowed any calculus lesson or Honors English quiz. I was receiving a dual education, one of books and higher learning, the other of street survival and decorum. The latter would follow me into my career choice of being a federal agent, as would a chance to come back years later and personally deal with many of the same assholes who laid siege to my school in the early 1980s.

After going to college and pursuing several meaningless jobs (including a four-year stint in baseball's minor leagues), I opted for the Bureau of Alcohol, Tobacco and Firearms in the late 1980s, primarily because it was the lead gang agency at the time. I didn't aspire to be a policeman, for I wanted to specialize in something. Specialization tasks or duties can take many years to attain with local departments, something I didn't want to wait for. Thus came ATF.

Though its history stemmed from Prohibition with illegal whiskey and tax evasion, ATF was then the premier gang-fighting agency. DEA was more concerned with the big drug organizations and dealers, the Pablo Escobars and Mexican Mafia chiefs. The FBI, well, the FBI was the FBI. ATF was the opposite; we were the bottom rung of the federal law enforcement ladder, but our main duty was to assist local agencies, and to these departments the street gangbanger was the biggest blip on their radar for his ruthlessness and indiscriminate use of violence.

It always pays to know someone, and luckily I knew several people in ATF. Without their assistance, I know my employment packet would never have made it to the top of the pile, and I am forever grateful to these individuals. I knew I had what it took to be an agent; politics, however, sometimes has other plans – as does the federal government. This would really emerge over my years as a Special Agent.

The only true prerequisites for ATF employment was a four-year degree (it could have been in Basket Weaving; I had majored in Political Science with an emphasis on Nuclear Weaponry and Foreign Policy) as well as a passing score on a standardized test put out by the Department of the Treasury. The test I passed – only barely – and thanks to my connections I was able to secure an interview. Though I didn't know it that day, I was to be hired.

During the interview process, one was asked to rank five cities of preference for assignment. I chose Los Angeles first, and was fairly confident I would get it. As stated, L.A. was ground zero of the gang problem, and I had made it quite evident in my applicant interview that that was why I was joining. I can't even remember the other cities I chose, though I think San Diego was one of them. I knew if I stayed in California I'd be able to work gangs to some extent. At the time the ATF Los Angeles Field Division also encompassed Arizona (Phoenix and Tucson), and if I had been stationed there I would have gone in a heartbeat.

But L.A. became my station. I was put in the Los Angeles Metro Group, which I would learn was an honor, for it was the main kick-ass group in the city. I would also be partnered up with all kinds of characters, young and old. The first year I swore I'd learn as much as I could from this spectrum of criminal investigators. Each agent had his own specialty, and I tried to glean something from each one of them – something I think I accomplished. These folks became my best friends, and after twenty years in the Bureau, they still remain the best agents I ever worked with, hands down. There were few attitudes, and mostly just an overall sense and effort to want to put assholes behind bars. And these assholes were gangbangers: Crips, Bloods, Hispanic gangs, Asian gangs, prison gangbangers recently back on the street – exactly the type of hoods I wanted to go after. Los Angeles, like New York City, held the unwritten title of being the major leagues of federal law enforcement in terms of types of criminal, violence, danger, and all the spoils that came with it.

Looking back, and somewhat ironically, today I wouldn't even consider the Bureau as a choice in my top 100 would-be professions. ATF has become an agency run by fools who hire robots whose sole duty is to rat-out fellow employees and maintain a low (or *no*) profile. Today putting criminals in jail has only become a by-product of ATF, no longer the product. And that's a shame. This book examines this travesty in depth.

The day I was hired I was given credentials, a badge, a gun, a pager, a car, and $20 to buy a holster. That was all. Today new agents receive everything from nifty equipment, raid outfits, hats, shirts, flashlights, golf shirts, mugs – you name it. Not only that, but new agents expect these accoutrements when they get hired. I didn't expect shit; I just wanted to hit the street and make an impact. The jury's still out on whether or not I or ATF had any impact, but I assure you I did touch many lives – both good and bad.

This book chronicles that history as well as a firsthand witnessing of an agency's slow demise.

Part One

Lost Angeles

I love livin' in the city - **FEAR**

You see us comin' and you all together run for cover - **PANTERA**

Chapter I

Boot

I'll always remember my first day working for ATF. After waiting nearly a year and working three jobs, I received a phone call asking if I'd be ready to start work for ATF the following Monday; thank God I was granted an additional two weeks before starting. At the time I lived 75 miles from the office, which was housed in the old Federal Building on Los Angeles Street in downtown LA. I would drive this 150-mile daily commute for six months before I was finally able to relocate my family to the city.

On arriving at ATF at 8:30 A.M. sharp that first day, dressed in a suit, I met the person who would become a second mother to me. Her name was Martha, and she was the Administrative Assistant/Secretary for the Los Angeles Metro Group. I had learned early in life that administrative folks can be your best friends or your worst enemies; it all hinged on your treatment of them. Throughout my career I treated the staff with the utmost respect, affection and many times with love. They are the backbone of ATF, and unfortunately they don't get a tenth of the appreciation they deserve.

I was about as green as they come, but getting to know Martha took no effort at all. She was an angel who treated me warmly and helped me whenever I needed it. I was shown about the office, met some of the other agents, and basically filled out tons of administrative paperwork that a new hire is required on his/her first day.

I soon learned that the agents in the office – seven or eight in all plus a supervisor – were pretty much on their own schedule. Each was required to put in ten hours per day, and our boss didn't really care what those hours were, as long as you kept to them and put people in jail. I liked this atmosphere.

In the office you had all kinds: old guards, new recruits, semi-new recruits, and those driven by the desire to do their job. The office reminded me of a factory, with multiple gears, wheels, and cogs working in perfect unison. Actually, there were few machines in the office (e.g., three agents usually shared one computer), but the ambience radiated professionalism, mechanical precision, and the ultimate desire to get the job done.

Every new agent is assigned a training officer, or "TO," on his/her first day. My TO, I soon learned from my boss and Martha, was an agent named Haley*. Haley usually got to the office around 11 A.M., but his quality hours came after dark. As I learned from him and many others in Metro, the hard-ass criminals usually didn't get out of bed until two or three in the afternoon, so coming into the office every morning at seven or eight – unless you had court or had tons of paperwork to get done – made little sense.

When I met Haley I was impressed for many reasons. First and foremost, he wore a tee shirt and jeans to work. I was green and believed I had to dress to impress, but Haley made it clear we weren't the FBI. I would soon learn that perpetrators we worked didn't respond to monkey suits.

Second, Haley was a big imposing guy. The joke was that he always wore a tee shirt two sizes too small to highlight his gigantic arms even though he didn't have to – he still would have looked massive in a triple-X tee. Also, Haley (I soon learned) was the premier undercover agent in the group, if not in the whole field division. Other groups were always asking for his services: first, because of his calm and composed demeanor; second, because of his size; and third, because he had the uncanny ability to change his appearance and "blend in" with anyone – professional *or* criminal. To this day I don't know his true lineage, but Haley had the rare talent of being able to work Black gangs, Hispanic gangs, prison gangs (he had previously worked in a prison and knew the jailhouse lexicon), and just about anyone else. He cast a huge shadow wherever he went, both literally and figuratively, and everyone in the group looked up to him – me most of all. Over the months and years he would become my greatest mentor, supporter, and friend. What I owe to him would take another book.

Over the course of my first weeks Haley would show me the rounds of ATF. He would also introduce me to other agents from other groups, most notably the best workers and the people for whom you would dive in front of a bus. At the time the Los Angeles Field Division had seven metropolitan groups, and anytime there was an enforcement operation, such as a search warrant, an ATF "All-Star Team" of the best and most trusted agents was usually used as the entry team. No arrogance or overconfidence – just an inimitable swagger that few could copy successfully. These all-stars also became my mentors and my best friends in the agency; they remain so to this day.

As I will elaborate on later, ATF personnel change dramatically when you go to a new field office or even field division. Los Angeles at the time was the Major Leagues of ATF, along with New York, Detroit, and maybe Boston. I felt extremely gratified to be getting my schooling from these veterans. Here's an example.

One day one of the old guards of the office, Starbuck*, took several of us "boots," as new hires were called, out to lunch. We drove around for what seemed like an eternity before Starbuck finally turned down a small forgotten street in East Los Angeles and cut the engine. None of us had any idea what was happening. At that point Starbuck turned around to the two or three of us in the backseat of his sedan and asked a fair question, "Okay, where are we?" The three of us looked at each other stupidly and then at the surrounding area, just trying to find a street sign. None was to be found – something very common in the inner city. No one answered his question. It was then that Starbuck said something I never forgot. He asked us, "What if we had just been in a shooting? I'm bleeding from the temple and one of you has to get on the radio and call for help. What are you going to say?" Again, no one had the answer, though the lesson was learned.

From that day forward I always knew where I was physically – at work or at any time, and over the years this would become the first thing I would teach my trainees: know your city. It can save your life and maybe someone else's. Over the years, and especially in other field offices, I learned how few agents adhered to this seemingly obvious credo. Like me and the other new boots in the car that day, no one mentored would ever forget that valuable lesson.

Starbuck also taught us another valuable lesson that day: never wear a seatbelt in the 'hood, for it may get you killed. At first I didn't get it, but after explanation it made perfect sense. In a unexpected firefight, unbuckling your seatbelt is the last thing you're going to think of. This also became my standard operating procedure (SOP).

I soon learned that LA Metro's specialty was gang enforcement, narcotics trafficking, and the illicit possession/trafficking of firearms. Recent federal legislation had been enacted mandating minimum/mandatory sentences for criminals, specifically using or carrying a firearm during a drug trafficking crime (a minimum 5-year sentence), as well as a "three-strike" rule (minimum 15-year sentence). It soon became obvious that almost every perpetrator qualified.

I'm not sure if it's a fact in every major city, but for some reason nearly every male adult that walked the streets of Los Angeles in the early 1990s had a felony record. Many were multiple-convicted felons. Whether or not this says something about the California justice system, is a separate subject altogether; let's just say it made my job easier. Also, nearly all of these felons possessed firearms. Understandable, living in the city. Yet, it was still against the law.

In the early 1990s there was no criminal background check for purchasing a firearm. California did have a 14-day waiting period, but instead of deterring the rash criminal from going in and buying a gun and then committing a crime immediately, the 14-day rule gave the criminal at least two weeks of malice aforethought. As Haley explained, certain firearms were more common among gang members than others.

The tools of the gangbanger trade were the AK-47 assault rifle, the Ruger Mini-14 rifle and the MAC-10/11 semi-automatic pistol. Machineguns were also in high demand, though procuring these was trickier, especially in California. Twelve gauge shotguns were also popular, especially sawed-off, which provided more spray and concealment. And of course there were cheap little pistols – the starter kit for perps-to-be. Our evidence vault contained hundreds if not thousands of these types of weapons, while the police had nothing to match this firepower.

Haley was close with several firearms dealers in south central Los Angeles, and usually when someone "suspicious" came in to buy a gun, he would be called. It doesn't take a brain surgeon to pick out who's suspect and who's not, though this type of "profiling" would be frowned upon in the coming decades. I can truthfully attest that there wasn't one person we "profiled" who wasn't up to something. Not one.

Unfortunately, the areas worked were not as racially integrated as they are today, so on paper it would appear we were targeting certain racial groups. That was, emphatically, not the case. I didn't draw up the south central LA demographic; I only enforced the laws.

When purchasing a firearm, the buyer had to fill out a federal form, called an ATF Form 4473, Firearms Transaction Record. This form would list personal information (date of birth, address, etc.) as well as the type(s) of firearms purchased. There was also a form called the Multiple Sales Form, which the gun dealer was required to complete should anyone purchase two or more handguns within any five-day span. These two forms were good tools for ATF agents; so, my early days on the job involved Haley and I going through hundreds of forms to see who was buying what. We developed many federal cases this way. We would subsequently do criminal history checks on suspicious purchasers, and as mentioned earlier, most of our "clientele" in LA were convicted felons. Since it was and is federally illegal for a convicted felon to have a firearm, it was like "shooting fish in a barrel."

We would subsequently get an arrest warrant and usually an accompanying search warrant to find the suspect and recover the firearm(s). The resulting enforcement operation would almost always recover the weapons in question as well as many more, including ammunition. Of all my days in Los Angeles I can think of only one instance where we didn't recover a firearm; that's a fairly good success rate considering the hundreds of warrants we executed in the early 1990s.

I also learned from seasoned vets how to prepare for warrant executions. One of my office mates introduced me to the Los Angeles Police Department's Air Support Division (ASD). ASD consisted of around 20 helicopters that LAPD had in its fleet – a small air force – and anyone who knows Los Angeles is familiar with the sound of choppers in the air at all hours of the day and night.

My first time up in the sky was memorable in that I was only accompanying a professional photographer employed to snap aerial photographs of over twenty warrant locations that we were to execute in the coming weeks. The photographer had the addresses and the pilot knew where to go; I just sat in the front passenger seat and ate up the experience.

Maybe "ate" wasn't a good choice of words, for we hadn't been airborne ten minutes when the photographer began to get sick. . . really sick. Thank God there was a throw-up bag on the ship, but after a short time it became apparent to all that this guy couldn't look through his lens finder without blowing chunks. As a result (and after landing at an LAPD substation), I traded places with the guy and became the photographer. It was a blessing in disguise because that day I learned how to take pictures from above.

I began to fly with ASD on a regular basis – at least once per week – in order to take aerial photographs of locations we would subsequently serve with search warrants. Since the sight of these choppers was an everyday occurrence all over LA, no one in the 'hood thought it strange for a helicopter to be circling above his/her city block. He/she probably would have thought it strange if *no* choppers were in sight.

I loved going up with ASD. Most of the pilots were ex-helicopter pilots who had served in Vietnam, and all of them were great guys. Moreover, on several occasions my photographic sessions were interrupted in order to respond to a chase or other problem on the ground. These excursions were awesome!

I knew I was doing something I loved.

Another valuable lesson I learned from seasoned agents was how to search a residence during a search warrant. No one is the be-all, end-all of searchers, though many people claim to be. I tried to learn something on every search warrant I assisted.

Criminals are not as dumb as you think, and they will hide contraband just about anywhere, including inside themselves. Some spots were borderline genius. For example, we would search cars often. One wouldn't normally think about popping the hood – at least I didn't – but you'd be surprised what you can find in an engine block or air filter compartment. We'd find handguns, dope, sawed-off shotguns – you name it – under the hoods of some of these cars.

Moreover, the home provided a multitude of hiding places. Since our warrants usually provided for narcotic searches, we basically had carte blanche to tear the place to pieces – something we did on occasion.

One search warrant provided another important lesson not in the ATF Directives. We were conducting a search at the residence of a rogue LAPD officer, a guy who was converting semi-automatic rifles to machineguns, or fully-automatic fire. We searched his house for hours but found nothing. The scene was tense (I never liked doing other cops), with LAPD Internal Affairs there as well as a host of supervisors.

During the warrant execution there was one ATF agent, Howard, who kept staring at a grate that sat in a hallway. This intake duct was screwed into the wall, and didn't appear to have ever been removed. Howard didn't care. Because we had found nothing, he just couldn't take his eyes off that vent. Finally he grabbed a screwdriver and began to remove the grate. Sure as hell there were three or four machineguns hidden in the passageway. I never went on a subsequent warrant where all grates weren't removed.

After being on the job several months I was shipped off to the Federal Law Enforcement Training Center (FLETC) in Brunswick, Georgia. At the time ATF sent new agents to two separate 8-week academies: the first was Criminal Investigator School (CIS) which was comprised of new special agents from many different agencies; and second, New Agent Training (NAT) which was strictly new ATF agents. I did in fact learn a lot at both sessions, especially on the law, but I knew my real schooling would come on the streets of Los Angeles.

My attendance at NAT was sadly marred by the death of a close friend, an ATF agent, who had been a classmate in CIS. His name was Brad Brown, and he was originally scheduled to be in my NAT class, but was bumped up to the class before mine. That was cool because I still got to hang out with him for several weeks where our classes overlapped. If only he had been in my class.

Three or four weeks after Brad returned to his post of duty in Sacramento, tragedy struck. Brad was sitting in the office one day missing home (he was from Michigan) and his fiancée – a nice young girl I had met and got to know during her visits to FLETC to see Brad. I wasn't in the Sacramento office during the episode, but the story went like this: somehow Brad's training officer put a gun to Brad's head as a joke, in Russian roulette fashion, and the gun went off. Brad was killed instantly.

I will remember it forever when our NAT curator took our whole class into one of the dorm rooms and told us of Brad's death. We were stunned to say the least, but not just for Brad. ATF lost two good agents that day, for his training officer ended up going to prison for five years for the shooting.

Lesson to be learned that day: don't ever screw around with guns, especially in the office. Yet, this wasn't the first or the last time a firearm would be discharged in the office.

It may have been before NAT, but I was an actual witness to an agent firing his duty weapon in the office; the incident occurred at the Van Nuys (CA) field office. I don't remember why I was there, but it was the first and last time I've ever set foot in that place. It was early in the morning and as far as I know every agent was in the office, as was the secretary. I was sitting at a small table in the middle of the squad-room, and next to me a new agent like myself – an ex-Marine – was being taught how to speedload his revolver by his training officer. No one was paying attention, but everyone hit the deck when the new agent fired a round at a huge tape spool which rested on top of a file cabinet.

After the shot and the smoke had cleared it got very, very quiet. I dove under the table and could only look on in disbelief. Had the agent's aim been only a few feet to the right he would have killed the secretary who sat at her desk down the hall.

Nobody knew what to say, but it was a senior agent who offered up these interesting words: "Okay, *this* does not leave here." I shook my head in total bewilderment and uttered under my breath, "Yeah, right!" I don't remember if the new agent was suspended for this, but he *and* his T.O. should have been. Again, the lesson to be learned: don't mess with guns anywhere! Unfortunately, as I would see over the course of my career, such accidental discharges were frequent occurrences. So were non-accidental discharges.

Shootings on the street were also a common occurrence in Los Angeles. In fact, ATF agents were involved in a shooting the very night I was on a flight to the ATF Academy for NAT. A good friend of mine and fellow agent was wounded, but the criminal got the worst of the exchange. He was shot in the balls with a shotgun. And he lived! I might have packed it in with that injury.

Through my whole career I never had to fire my gun during an enforcement operation, and I am very proud of that. There were many times when I could have shot, but having no law enforcement or military experience, I could only rely on my ATF training, and that regimentation was one of the best things I got from ATF. The closest I came to pulling the trigger was on a very late night in the infamous Rampart division of LAPD.

The operation involved an undercover ATF agent purchasing a small amount of narcotics from an apartment in a multi-story building. Rampart has become synonymous over the years with drugs, pimps, whores, and just about everything else, and as a result we had many support cars in the area should something go wrong with the undercover transaction. The dope sale went as planned; the problem occurred when one of the support cars was shot at by a car containing gangbangers who controlled that section of the Rampart area. Apparently the gangsters thought it strange that two people should be sitting in their car with the motor running and doing nothing. A short gun battle ensued between both cars before the gangster car sped off.

Haley and I were positioned in the ATF surveillance van monitoring via radio the electronic transmitter on the undercover agent. We also had an LAPD officer with us who sat in the back of the van. Our sole duty that night was to record the drug buy and then follow the undercover agent out of the area and to safety after the transaction was made. This was done with precision, but no sooner had we deposited the undercover at his car when the radio traffic began spewing forth. Chico* (the agent I would learn later was in the car fired upon) called out over the air the description of the shooter vehicle as well as its direction of travel. Apparently the car was a Nissan 280ZX or similar model with heavy splotches of bondo, or putty repair patches, all over the hood. Direction of travel was eastbound which was in the direction of the skyscrapers of downtown LA.

As radio traffic continued to come, Haley and I knew we were well out of the game. The suspect car was heading towards East LA and we were probably miles from the action. I took no chances however and grabbed my .223 caliber Colt AR-15 rifle and sat down in the front passenger seat next to Haley. The LAPD cop stayed in the back of the van and monitored LAPD radio traffic. Haley in turn put the van in drive and we began driving eastbound, knowing full well that if anyone else was going to get in a shooting that night, it wasn't us.

After about three minutes we were driving eastbound on San Marino Street when I noticed a car in the distance coming at us with its lights off. Remarkably visibility was good that night (unlike other areas of LA) and I quickly realized that the car coming westbound matched the description of the shooter's vehicle. A perfect match. Moreover, the auto was driving at an excessive amount of speed – obviously trying to get away from something or someone.

I alerted Haley and told him to try to run the car off the road. Our van had slowed down tremendously and Haley tried to ease the van to the left to force the fleeing vehicle onto the sidewalk or into some parked cars. Meanwhile, I levied my rifle out of Haley's driver's side window and prepared to shoot up the car as it made its way past us. The police officer in the back we could have cared less about; I forgot he was even there despite his shouting in opposition to my brilliant idea.

It became nail-biting time, and as I began to squeeze the trigger the car flew past us and out of sight for the evening. It was gone. It's a good thing Haley didn't bump the escaping vehicle because I would have been jettisoned out of the windshield like a human cannon ball. The guy in back probably would have suffered the same fate. After gathering in what had just happened, I quickly got on the air and told all parties that the vehicle in question was not heading towards East Los Angeles, but was rather heading westbound to points unknown. In other words, the car was in the wind.

One thing I'll always admire about the Los Angeles Police Department (there are too many to recount in this book) is that when one of its officers is involved in a shooting and the perpetrator escapes, the whole Department circles its wagons and basically shuts down all other police business until the assholes are caught. This was no exception. The cover car that was shot at had contained an LAPD officer and ATF agent Chico. Little did I know that I would play a huge role in the aftermath of the shooting.

After the melee, hundreds of tips began pouring in from just about everywhere. Apparently the shooter was part of a Central American street gang that was just beginning to make its presence felt in California. It was also believed that the gangbanger had been wounded. All of us stayed up for over two days pounding the streets to find the shooter and the car. The car. There were only four people who had seen the car: Chico, the LAPD officer, Haley, and me. The cop, as is LAPD policy, was immediately put on three-day's administrative absence and was out of the picture. Chico became inundated by the post-shooting review, puzzled supervisors, and an uncaring, pissed off wife at home who could only harangue about Chico not getting home for supper. No, I'm not joking.

That left Haley and me.

I believe it was the second day after the shooting – no one had slept for days – but Haley and I, along with two other agents were told by LAPD to go sit on a house in El Monte (east of LA) because the residence had ties to the possible suspect. Seemed like a longshot, but the four of us made the twenty minute drive east and set up a good vantage point on a single-story house in a decent neighborhood. We weren't sure how long we'd be sitting in that residential area, but we planned for the worst.

Unbelievably, we hadn't been in position more than an hour before a light 280ZX with putty stains all over the hood pulled into the driveway. I radioed to my supervisor, who was with us, that that was indeed the car we had seen two nights before. And so we waited. As soon as the car left the house, we all performed a felony car stop on the vehicle and arrested the suspect without incident. My boss called the suspect out of the car (he was the passenger; his girlfriend was driving) and instructed him to walk backwards towards us. The Hispanic male wore no shirt but was tattooed heavily across his back with the name of his street gang – the very gang we had been working two nights before.

I knew this was the asshole. Haley quickly moved up behind the suspect and handcuffed him.

Not only was he the right suspect, but there were bullet holes on the passenger side of the 280ZX as well as bloodstains. I felt extremely proud of this operation (as was LAPD), and I think the guy subsequently was sent to prison for 12 years. Not a bad hit. I only wonder if the guy realized how close he came to being shot by me that night with my .223. Lucky for him.

I was present during several operations that involved shootings, and all were righteous and no one was killed, but the stress that comes with the post-shooting investigation is immeasurable. Chico can attest to this after the episode described above.

After any shooting (whether by an agent, policeman, or perpetrator) ATF sends out a formal Shooting Review Team. This usually includes a Special Agent in Charge (SAC) from another field division, Internal Affairs, and a team of outside investigators. Some reviews went well, others not so much. It all depended on the review team personnel.

I witnessed many special agents get grilled by a not-so-understanding investigator, almost to the point of tears. As I said, I was never involved in a shootout that wasn't a good shoot, though many investigators viewed all shootings as suspect. It was as though the agent or cop became the suspect while the criminal got away.

Notwithstanding, we (ATF) led the nation in shootings for many years – not because we were trigger-happy, but because we went after the baddest of the bad. Also, there were several occasions when we were shot at and no review team was summoned. We figured if we didn't know where the firing was coming from, then it wasn't worth the hassle to call in a review team who would only question the agents on why they were at a particular location on a particular evening. Many times there was no answer to that question; we were just out and about looking for the shit.

One time I was patrolling the streets and my car took a round/ricochet right on the small door that covers the gas cap. I felt the car take the hit, and when I subsequently inspected the vehicle I saw where the paint had come off on the door. It wasn't much more than a scratch, and though I thought about calling my boss and reporting the episode, I figured, "no harm no foul." Who needs all the paperwork? I just went about my enforcement operation. That night was memorable, for now I had even more of an ax to grind.

Here's another example. Common enforcement venues were the multiple housing projects in south central Los Angeles. For some reason these two- or three-story tenement rows carried the pleasant names "Gardens" or "Courts," but all were extremely dangerous places. They were almost always peopled by the lowest socioeconomic order, tons of kids who played in the street throughout the night, and gangbangers. Many of the apartments were connected by hidden passageways used to elude police officers or anyone else.

I made it a point to stay out of the residences as much as I could. Most of our enforcement activities took place outside where the gangsters would congregate and keep watch over their turf. One night sticks with me forever.

While we were in one of these garden spots, a fellow agent was just standing around keeping watch. At some point he noticed a reddish stain on his bullet-proof vest (we ALWAYS wore vests), but when he attempted to brush it off, it wouldn't budge. It just stayed there. After a while another agent came up to him and asked what he was doing because he could see his partner becoming annoyed. When the other agent got close he saw what his partner was doing, but he could only look on in horror. On his friend's chest, right over the ATF patch, was a laser beam pointed straight at the heart. Where it originated from no one knew. No one cared at this point. We could only get the hell out of there before something truly tragic happened. These were the types of criminals and places we worked.

Thus, after receiving my academy schooling as well as my hands-on education (thanks to my fellow agents who knew more than I did), it would soon be time for me to branch out on my own. After a certain amount of time one's training officer and boss grant the new agent some independence to work his or her own investigations. Thanks to Haley's tutelage, I had become well-schooled in ATF paperwork, court appearances, preparing warrants and complaints, as well as cementing myself as someone anyone could rely on. Whenever I got a call to be somewhere, I would be there. But now it was time to do what I had joined ATF to do. It was to have all the makings of a wild-west show, but that adrenaline rush was something I lived for.

Now it was time.

Chapter II

Enter the Dragon

Hazing of new agents goes back at least to the 1930s, and I've heard various outlandish stories from around the nation, some bordering on legend, some *urban* legend.

In Los Angeles we had several routines, but a night spent at 7th Street and Central Avenue in downtown LA was an all-timer. It usually began as we were mopping up or finishing cruising the streets, and it always was well into the morning hours.

For some reason that intersection attracted some of the most indescribable human beings (if that's what they were) one would ever see. It was as if the sewer covers just popped open at the witching hour and these creatures crawled out to compare and strut their wares, like a scene out of *Escape From New York* or the bar scene in *Star Wars*.

You had all kinds of dudes walking around, but these weren't your ordinary "fellas." In fact, they were all drag queens, dressed to the tits (pun intended) and out for a hot night on the town – or at least at this intersection. These weren't your ordinary "dragons " (as we called them); many looked like actual females. So we always got a kick out of seeing how a new agent would react when seeing these "guys."

The Los Angeles Field Division had agents from all over the country, so it wasn't just the new "green" agents who were taken down to 7th and Central. I had been taken down here by Haley and some other veterans in my early days, but having spent a good deal of time in downtown LA and Hollywood (my father had been an actor), I knew a dragon when I saw one. Other agents weren't as worldly.

One particular hazing was played on a veteran agent. We had just finished working for the night and decided to take agent Don* out for a short sight-seeing tour. Don, who had the nickname Richochet Rabbit after the cartoon character, was a good guy but very energetic – a likely candidate for the chicanery we had in mind. When he asked where he was being taken we only told him we were going to check out the local prostitutes who were known to walk the streets in the area.

No one ever objected to that.

On arrival, the corner and adjoining block was rife with activity – prostitutes, pimps, drug dealers, and of course the aforementioned dragons. One in particular immediately caught Don's eye. "She" wore a low-cut dress, high heels, tons of make-up and pictured herself the next Veronica Lake. As we drove by she motioned us to U-turn and come back and I quickly complied.

Don was in the passenger seat and could only hoot and holler about how that chick was pretty hot for being a lady-of-the-night. Of course we all agreed. There were four of us in the vehicle, and the three of us who were in on the joke had to be composed and control our laughter.

As the dragon got close, Don starting talking to her. She really did look female; she had the voice, a bust-line, and a fairly decent figure. As Don kept talking to her, the dragon slowly raised her arms up over her head, revealing more underarm hair than a gorilla. Don's face dropped to the floor, and the rest of us could only burst out in uncontrollable laughter.

He then realized he'd been had and quickly told me to get the hell out of there, of which I did amid the din of laughter emanating from the car. Don could only shake his head and chuckle as well. He took it well and enjoyed the laugh as much as the rest of us. It was a classic scene! He should be thankful that's all he was shown; many times we got the full dress lift-up.

Other hazed agents weren't as self-effacing or content with being fooled. Some we literally had to stop from jumping out of the car and beating the living shit out of one of these pretenders. Most of us saw it as fun, for the dragons were harmless, but some agents didn't like to be the butt of someone else's joke.

This attitude usually reflected their performance as agents. Hell, these queens probably were making more money than all of us at the time.

Nice rule – always be careful on whom you judge.

Chapter III

Hell Comes To Your House

Andrew Vita – Andy – was the ATF Special Agent in Charge (SAC) of the Los Angeles Field Division (LAFD) when I was hired. He hired many ex-athletes, from lacrosse to track to football to baseball – in which I happened to be an ex-infielder looking for a job.

Vita knew the discipline that was integral to athletics. He understood camaraderie and teamwork, and I think he played some baseball in his day. He knew that a competitive countenance was important in a new agent, and for the most part his hires turned out to be some of the best.

I can also attest that he was a tough son of a bitch. Example: He, I, and some other ATF agents played in a softball tournament around 1991, and in one game in particular Andy got a hit and made it to second base. The next batter belted a single to the outfield and Andy scored. Sliding – in only shorts! He just got up, dusted himself off, and walked to the dugout with blood running profusely down his leg. I had suffered many a "strawberry" in my days in the minor leagues – terrible, bleeding skin abrasions suffered from sliding into bases. I still have scars. Andy's wound looked pretty serious, but he just brushed it off and the game went on. That was Andy.

Unfortunately, Andy Vita's tenure in Los Angeles was short. He was a "climber" and he went on to have a very fruitful career with ATF, as did his Assistant Special Agent in Charge (ASAC) Robert Wahl. These guys were good dudes – men who understood the mission of putting people in jail. Vita's successor, however, was exactly the opposite and not what the LAFD needed to fill the vacuum. In fact, when Lenny Sandoval* took over as SAC his first order of business was to hold an all-hands meeting of the agents in the Los Angeles Field Division. He had come from somewhere in the Midwest and he had an ultimatum to the troops: "I don't want any cowboys in my field division." That was his credo. Period.

Many of us just looked at each other in astonishment. Boy, we said to one other, did this guy sure come to the wrong city! We went about our business anyway and with a vengeance.

Sandoval would figure later, albeit ignominiously, in the Los Angeles Riots of 1992.

Now that I could work cases independently without Haley (though I referenced his knowledge and street-savvy almost daily), I set about to do what I had joined the Bureau to do, and that was to target a specific gang. My sights had always been set to return to the area of my old high school, but around this time I was assigned to a task force that worked jointly with the Newton Street Division precinct of the Los Angeles Police Department. "Shootin' Newton," as it was called, was one of the hairiest areas in all LA. It was a hodgepodge of Crips, Bloods, Hispanic gangs, and other territorial gangsters. Many of these gangs were already being worked by other agents in the task force, so I decided to pick a gang and turf that was virgin territory. Those unlucky bastards were the Seven-Deuce (72) East Coast Crips*. Many gangs in the Newton area affixed the surname East Coast Crips (ECC) because their territories fell on the east side of the Harbor Freeway which runs from downtown LA all the way to the Port of San Pedro. The 72 ECC were known for the usual shenanigans: drug trafficking, murder, extortion, everything. They seemed like as good a target as any.

It also helped that I had several informants who lived in the area. I didn't ask much from these brave and money-motivated people – only that they point out which houses in the two block area sold drugs and guns. Narcotics was our main ticket to getting search warrants for these homes. We would send an informant up to the door of the house, buy crack cocaine, and then get a search warrant for the home.

Sometimes we would just sit in the area (an extremely dangerous activity) and watch a house. Surveillance of these residences was like watching the front door of a Circle K mini-market. The foot traffic was unbelievable. Documentation of this unusual popularity would also be used to get search warrants.

Now, getting federal warrants was not the optimal practice; it would usually take a week or longer to get "federal paper," if the Assistant US Attorneys would even listen to you. Instead we procured state search warrants. They were faster to obtain (we needed to move quickly because many of these dope houses were "here today, gone tomorrow"), and there wasn't a lot of scrutiny given by the district attorneys or the state judges. In fact, with a state warrant we didn't have to deal with any attorneys, which was a plus.

Also, getting a state warrant didn't require as much probable cause as the US Attorney's Office required, which usually encompassed a series of narcotics purchases out of the house, endangering the confidentiality of your informant. With the state, one purchase out of the house was enough, and we took advantage of this.

I can truthfully say we never hit a house that wasn't involved in illicit activity, though many federal attorneys would have put us through the ringer to "get paper" for a house. So we neglected them altogether. We knew that we would find spoils that would then push us into the federal arena where the federal prosecutors couldn't say no, but our calling card was a state search warrant.

In the span of nearly two years I must have written search warrants for nearly every house on those two blocks controlled by the 72 ECC. Some homes we hit more than once. We also developed another calling card, and this went back to my punk rock days. In 1981 a compilation album of local LA punk bands was released under the name *Hell Comes To Your House*. It featured such up-and-coming bands as Social Distortion, 45 Grave, and Legal Weapon – ironic and fitting band names to say the least. Great music! On the cover of the album was this devilish looking guy, standing in front of a door, and holding two sticks that were set ablaze. I subsequently hung the album cover (yes, *album*, for I had the record on vinyl) on the wall behind my desk at the task force office. It became my personal verbal calling card, reminiscent of Robert Duvall putting death cards on dead Vietcong in *Apocalypse Now*.

Every warrant that followed went like this. We would knock and announce at the front door by identifying who we were and why we were there. Then, an agent who I dubbed "Easton Patrol" (named after the aluminum bat I kept from my college baseball days) would bash out the bathroom window; this would preclude anyone inside from rushing to the toilet to flush evidence. There were several times when someone was actually sitting on the pot; boy, did he/she get a surprise! When no one answered the front door after 8-10 seconds (which was the case 95% of the time), we would then breach the door and do our entry. Once inside I would then utter the famous words (or *infamous*, if you happened to be in the place), "Hell comes to your house." To me it was a war and the only way to deal with these thugs, and I never lost sight of that. Nobody inside thought it was funny, but we got a short chuckle out of it.

Most warrant executions were non-eventful, i.e., no one got shot or killed; though, some were more memorable than others. One particular search warrant was classic. Our task force was racially-integrated, but as mentioned earlier, in the LAFD you could assemble an all-star entry team if so desired. For this warrant we had intelligence that there were some pretty big dudes inside the house. Therefore, I assembled my all-star team from all over the LAFD to do the entry: 8-10 monster agents who happened to be all black. Many were ex-football players who could crush a skull with one hand. The racial choice was just coincidental, but it had a funny outcome.

After these goliaths had made entry and secured the home, we brought all the residents outside and put them on the front lawn. After the house was safe for us to search, the entry team came outside to get a breath of *fresh* Los Angeles air. One of the perpetrators, seated on the lawn with his hands handcuffed behind his back, took one look at this federal "football team" and uttered the memorable words, "Man, I ain't never seen so many bruthas in a white man's army." We got a good laugh out of that. I guess hell can come to a man's house in many forms. This unfortunate prognosticator was soon transported to jail and did many years because of what we recovered in the home.

Another memorable time: we'd been looking at a certain upstairs apartment for some time and knew narcotics and guns were being sold out of it. I can't remember if we made a purchase out of the apartment or not, but we wanted to hit the site when all the perpetrators were present; otherwise, we would have a tough time pinning the illegal spoils on anyone. One of my partners Pedro*, a new agent, offered to sit in a van and do surveillance on the residence for many hours and let us know when would be the best time to hit the place.

What he noticed was a lot of foot traffic between the apartment and a single-story home located directly across the street. It appeared that the home was a "stash house", and that the apartment was only where the illicit sales took place. That way, even if the apartment got hit by the cops, then the stash house would be free and clear. Thanks to Pedro's keen eye, I was able to get search warrants for both residences.

The spoils were awesome: three criminals, multiple firearms, crack cocaine, and two kilograms of powder cocaine – a find we rarely came upon. This turned out to be one of the biggest hits of the task force, and three suspects received 40, 35, and 25 years of federal prison time respectively because of it. Had I been hasty (and I was at times), we never would have got the cocaine powder out of the stash house. A good agent can learn from anyone, and that day I learned from Pedro the Boot that a little extra surveillance can go a long way. Just ask the criminals.

Another house: this one we hit, it seemed, like every month. And to my astonishment, every warrant yielded illicit goods and usually new suspects. This particular time we had intelligence that there was one ex-con inside that, if given the chance, would run and probably shoot it out with the cops. So, we put several agents and police officers in the alley behind the house should anyone run out the back. I gave specific instructions to these officers that if anyone came out the back door, to be ready to shoot to kill because it was probably the main guy we were looking for.

As it turned out, my boss came along on the warrant execution. This was unusual, for he rarely ventured out with the task force. He had also been at the briefing and knew all the preliminary plans. But, for some reason he forgot the most important instruction and subsequently, upon entry, went barreling out the back of the house! Gun out, everything! To this day I don't know if he knows how close he came to getting shot, but I did professionally let him know at the debriefing.

Another funny aside to this warrant was that while we were searching the residence, another gangbanger who we knew happened to drive up and park in front of the home. During all searches subsequent to entry we would keep several agents and police officers outside to act as perimeter cover. This post was very dangerous, for local folks and assholes would almost always congregate outside to see what all the commotion was about – many times spray painting our vehicles in the process.

Inside the residence was a lot safer. It just so happened that inside the house we recovered a sawed-off 410 shotgun. As noted earlier, the 12 gauge was the gangbanger caliber of choice when it came to shotguns; so, this particular weapon was unique. But not unique to the guy who drove up and parked in front of the house. After getting consent to search his vehicle (permission we never had trouble obtaining), eight 410 shotgun shells were found in the guy's trunk. He thought nothing of it because it was just ammunition. Well, he was a convicted felon (like everyone) and it was illegal for him to possess ammunition as well as a firearm. So he was arrested for the ammunition, and since those eight rounds matched the gun we had found in the house, that poor bastard was given eight years by the presiding judge – one year for each round. Even in our circles that was a hell of a hit.

Note to others: when the cops are in your house and you are not present, stay the hell away; you never know what may happen.

Another interesting warrant site became known as the Circuit City of the Ghetto. This particular dude sold crack cocaine but was also a fence, so one could pay for the dope with televisions, computers, toasters, whatever. And yes, most of those bartered items were, as we say in police circles, a little "warm."

I subsequently got paper to hit the house and when we did we could barely walk in the place because of all the electronics. You name it, it was in there. During the raid we recovered multiple firearms and a large amount of crack cocaine; both occupants were arrested and subsequently wound up in federal court.

Now, we as federal agents didn't deal in stolen property (which we were sure all the stuff was), so after the warrant I let the place sit unoccupied for 24 hours before we notified LAPD Stolen Property Bureau. The next day I accompanied the latter detectives back to the site but something miraculous had happened. Every stereo, TV, car radio, computer, portable fridge, etc. had been removed from the house. It had to have been the biggest smash-and-grab in history of the new decade (this was before the LA Riots). The detectives and I could only laugh and feel somewhat relieved; no one really wanted to do the paperwork on that stuff anyway.

Another warrant location was funny for several reasons. We were looking for a particular gangbanger, a multi-convicted felon who was one of the main badasses of the 72 ECC, and it was his apartment that we had paper for. The residence was on the second story of a multi-unit building, and the front door sat at the end of a very tight and dimly-lit hallway. After knocking and announcing at the door (to which no one, go figure, answered), the decision to forcibly breach the door became our only option. Since the space to do so was limited, the person using the ram was unable to get much leverage in striking the pick, or hooligan tool, that was being held in place by another agent to breach the door. The agent with the ram – which weighed approximately fifty pounds of forged steel – missed the pick entirely and crushed the hand of the agent holding the pry tool. You could have heard the bones breaking down the block. Yet, the agent who sustained the hit didn't even shudder, for his adrenaline was going through the roof knowing that if someone was inside the apartment and wanted to shoot, then he was a dead man. I cringed when I saw the hand flattened, but we went in anyway after entry was finally made.

The minute we got inside we observed a black male dive out a window; he looked like the guy we were looking for, but it was dark and no one could really be sure. Somehow the guy got away, and to this day I don't know how he pulled that leap off without breaking both legs. His escape was only temporary however, for soon after, an agent in my office obtained a warrant for his arrest based on what we had "witnessed" that night. In other words, the guy doing the Tarzan rendition out of the window *became* the guy we were looking for, even if it wasn't him. The case was weak to say the least, but because the guy had such an extensive criminal record (and needed to be off the street), he was detained in federal lockup pending all subsequent criminal court proceedings. We didn't give a shit that the case would never make it through trial, and as a result we let him rot behind bars for four to six months before his indictment was eventually dismissed and he was released from federal custody. Hell really did come to this poor bastard's house – even if he hadn't been there.

Sometimes the joke was on us. One time Don*, aka Richochet Rabbit, had some intelligence (and I use that term lightly in this case) that a Mexican national fugitive was hiding out in a location east of Los Angeles. Apparently the suspect had assassinated a police officer in Mexico and made his way to LA. A common occurrence these days, but not so common back in the early 1990s. Don requested the assistance of the "Hell Comes to Your House" crew, and we were more than happy to oblige. Though Don had the habit of embellishing details and facts, he was a good investigator, so we took the assignment very seriously.

After a moderate drive we arrived at the apartment where the supposed fugitive was hiding. Don wanted to be low-key in encountering anyone at the residence, and we obliged. I can't remember what ruse was used, but it may have been the UPS trick; one of our agents had a UPS uniform in his car which served quite nicely as a ruse on many occasions. I personally kept a Domino's Pizza outfit handy (I had driven for them before joining ATF) and I never knew when it might be put to good use.

Don went up to the front door, and after some unintelligible talk, he dragged a short Hispanic male out to the cars and told us this was the person we had come to arrest. Problem was: this guy looked anything but an antigovernment assassin. First off, he was crippled; he could barely walk, but this didn't stop Don from tossing the guy around like a Frisbee. I personally inquired into the suspect's health, and Don said it was probably the result of the gunfight that ensued after the Mexican police officer had been killed.

I still had a hard time believing this was the true killer. I mean, the guy couldn't have weighed more than eighty pounds, could barely talk, and walked like Igor in the old *Frankenstein* movies. I holstered my opposition and told Don to put the guy in a car for transport downtown. Since I had the only large sedan in the posse, I was given this inauspicious duty. Unfortunately, this presented all kinds of problems. Due to the guy's disability, he couldn't be put in the front passenger seat, handcuffed, and therefore transported without being in severe pain. The backseat was out as well, but Don came up with a novel idea. He decided that since the suspect was most comfortable turned on his right side, Don would place the guy in the front passenger seat, have him hold his left arm out of the window and then handcuff that wrist to the suspect's right wrist which was to be suspended out of the backseat window. Trust me: I couldn't make this up if I tried.

Obviously the latter method was scrubbed, but this fiasco went on for a half hour. During the impasse it finally came to me who the suspect looked like. I returned to my childhood and could only see in front of me actor Burgess Meredith from the old *Batman* television series. It was he in the flesh.

Finally my patience gave out. I turned to Richochet and said indignantly, "Listen dude, put the fucking Penguin in the car and let's get the hell out of here." This got a huge laugh from the entire arrest team even though Don didn't see the humor (or maybe he didn't get the joke). After hearing my retort, Don walked up behind me and slapped me as hard as he could on my back. I turned around in shock, but you could have hit me with pound of molten lava at that point because I wanted blood. I was going to kill Don, and thanks to several co-workers, this second homicide didn't happen.

I don't remember how we got the Penguin downtown, but I do know that it turned out to be the wrong guy (of course!). Don was still livid over my less-than-professional demeanor during the episode, and he subsequently wrote me up in a memorandum which he submitted to our boss. That supervisor, Rodney, had been at the scene and knew Don's bullshit better than anyone. He just threw the memo in the garbage and life went on. I still don't know if the actual cop killer was found. I doubt it.

There are many more examples but too many to elaborate on here. Such was the evolution of Hell Comes To Your House. It's unclear whether or not SAC Sandoval had any idea what we were up to, but he had to be privy to the results. Our task force was kicking ass and taking names; so, Sandoval for the most part stayed out of our way. Besides, we were making him look good, which for a SAC is golden. Had he really known what our tactics were and the potential danger we were bringing to the Bureau (in terms of public relations), he turned a blind eye. Thankfully.

Yet, there were certain practices we were undertaking that would have made him piss his pants. "No cowboys in my division," he had once uttered. Well, the real wild-west showdowns came in the form of another enforcement activity, one that became the stuff of legend in the Los Angeles Field Division.

It was time to take it to the gangs head on, and we had just the mentality and desire to do so.

Chapter IV

Heavy Metal Interrogation Techniques

There are many training schools offered to the criminal investigator that deal with the fine art of interviewing/interrogation. Most are highly structured and base their philosophy on the unproven fact that the law enforcement officer is smarter than the criminal. That may be true in many scenarios, but the alert and proactive street cop never underestimates the psyche or intelligence of his prey. So, we at ATF came up with our own brand of soliciting information, albeit crude and perhaps Constitution-bending.

Much of the hip-hop culture grew alongside or in conjunction with the "gangsta" mentality. The music centered around urban commerce (i.e., narcotics trafficking, murder, and other stripe-earning activities), disdain for local law enforcement, and the casual yet caustic degradation of women. I've been a music connoisseur my entire life, though I don't subscribe to the lyrics and musical content (or lack thereof) of rap music. In fact, if you can make out five words of any song of the music I listen to, then you've got a trained ear. I don't even know what the hell is being said. I'm just in it for the guitars. Rap, on the other hand, is all about being lyrically heard and understood.

As stated earlier, I grew up in Los Angeles in the late 1970s and early '80s, which happened to be Ground Zero for the hardcore punk rock revolution that gripped the United States at that time. Bands like Black Flag, TSOL, DOA, Dead Kennedys, and a plethora of other guitar-driven bands were making their mark on many disenfranchised youths. I didn't see myself as disenfranchised, but the volume, speed, and musical precision converted me almost overnight. Many people (mostly parents – my own included) saw this brand of music as nothing more than noise and anarchistic drivel. Those of us involved in the scene's evolution knew differently, and because of this musical socialization I was able to employ this "noise" to my advantage in my days with ATF.

It usually started with the arrest of a gangbanger. Crips and Bloods were preferred but occasionally we'd try this technique on a Hispanic gang member. To the latter's credit (of which I bestow very little), the Hispanics for the most part thought the technique was funny, unless they were having a bad day. A really bad day meant being transported to the Metropolitan Detention Center (MDC) downtown knowing you were looking at 15 years to life in the federal can. Oh, the beauty of leverage.

But it was the black gangs with which we had the most success. It usually began with a roundabout route to MDC in the middle of the night. It didn't matter if you dumped the perpetrators off at 7 P.M. or 4 A.M.; you were still required to take them before a federal Magistrate Judge first thing the next morning. We also had a habit of "hooking" crooks on Friday nights because the suspect would have to spend the whole weekend in jail awaiting his First Appearance on Monday morning. Three-day weekends were even better occasions.

While en route to MDC we would coyly insert a cassette tape containing everything from Iron Maiden, Metallica, or any of the above-mentioned bands. As an added "treat" we would put the "red ball" (a portable spinning red lamp that had a magnet which you affixed to the top of the car or dashboard when in pursuit – immortalized in 1970s police dramas like *Kojak, Starsky & Hutch*, and *Barnaby Jones)* on the floorboard. So, with the volume pumped up to 11 and the red ball swirling around on the car floor, the prisoner transport vehicle miraculously transformed itself into a supersonic discothèque on wheels.

We would always transport the crooks in one car, closely followed by another car for protection. Those seated in the second car were treated to one of the funniest sights imaginable. Two agents, up front rocking out, and one to two criminals shackled in the backseat shaking their heads to the point of detachment. It was a scene straight out of the Kubrick classic *A Clockwork Orange.*

As a result (or maybe because they really did want to atone for their crimes), the gangbangers would usually tell us just about anything we wanted to hear to get the music turned off. Rest assured, it's pretty amazing what good music will elicit out of someone who doesn't want to talk and who doesn't necessarily think all the racket is music to the eardrums. Bad music's even better.

This may be stretching *Miranda* a little bit, but to compete in the war on the streets, sometimes the rules needed to be altered. A street cop and agent already has his hands tied behind his back due to the legal system (or lack thereof); we were just trying to even the playing field.

As I said above, thank Heaven for leverage.

Chapter V

Jackin'

Most of our work in south central Los Angeles was proactive though mundane: we initiated investigations, dealt with cases on our own terms, retrieved records, did lots of paperwork, and basically had a timeline that was more or less adhered to. Yet, we had another proactive tactic, one much more dangerous and spontaneous, and it involved just cruising the neighborhood looking for the *shit*. It became known as jackin'.

This became my ultimate payback to the gangs of Los Angeles and one that would have made our bosses cringe. In other words, they had no idea what we were doing late at night in the 'hood. Our cover story was simple enough: we just said we were out checking addresses or doing some non-dangerous surveillance. Nothing was further from the truth; we were taking the war to the gangbangers, those *angels* who had besmirched the name of the City of Los Angeles.

Jackin' usually involved two vehicles: optimally one "cool" car (i.e., a vehicle that didn't look like the police) with two agents, and a pursuit/jackin' vehicle (large sedan) with four agents. Sometimes it involved two large sedans with anywhere from six to eight agents. It also involved bullet-proof vests and shotguns and rifles, making our sidearms the last resort should shit go terribly awry. We knew the type of firepower the gangs possessed and this at least leveled the playing field. Plus, we had the element of surprise.

I drove a V-8 Ford Mustang 5.0. The car had saved my life on several occasions, but on a jackin' evening, my co-rider and I were usually the finders, the lookouts for gangbangers just hanging out on a street in their neighborhood. And, they weren't hard to find.

The tactic went like this: once the gangsters were located by the cool car, we would radio to the jackin' car and relay the gangbangers' location. We always communicated on a non-ATF radio frequency –

just in case any of the bosses happened to be listening to an ATF-band in the middle of the night.

Once the gangsters' locale was called out, the jackin' car would swoop in. Each agent would then jump out with shotgun and/or rifle and corner his prey. The orders were simple: first, runners (and there were usually a few) were allowed to escape; second (and this was most important), should any remaining gangbanger display any type of weapon with the intention of starting a firefight, the agents with the heavy artillery were instructed to shoot to kill.

This usually didn't have to be uttered, and this obviously meant the operation had to involve a special type of agent all-star team; everyone had to be completely trustworthy.

If no firefight ensued (and thankfully none did), the responding agents put everyone on the ground on their knees with their hands behind their heads. At this time all people were searched for weapons and paraphernalia.

The searches usually yielded all types of goodies: narcotics, drug paraphernalia, knives, feces in the gangster' pants, and occasionally firearms. Since the tactic stretched the Fourth Amendment (to put it lightly), those caught with contraband usually became informants to be utilized at later dates. The rush was indescribable, though it wasn't the result we ultimately sought. It's been said that only the foolhardy get hooked on adrenaline, and that's the truth. In terms of jackin', adrenaline was a by-product, not a product.

After some time, the gangs of Los Angeles began to know who we were – and they became scared of ATF. After a while, many gang members would completely scatter on seeing us; this was our desired effect. It went like clockwork, and we began to make a name for ourselves, albeit infamously.

Sometimes we'd become privy to a drive-by shooting nearly in progress. By *nearly*, I mean if we hadn't intervened some gangbanger (or more than one) would have become the shooting victim of a rival gangster in another car. Once the two "asshole" cars realized they were being pursued by an unknown third or fourth car (us), the gangster cars would try to escape. One usually did, but we would always be able to race down the other vehicle, throw on the police lights and siren, and pull the car over.

In these situations, guns were almost always recovered and the perpetrators taken to jail. Some would say this tactic stretched the Fourth Amendment as well, but we were basically witnesses to a crime in progress – usually attempted murder. Regardless, all these cases held up in court.

The pursuits were sometimes stories-in-themselves, and some even involved the agent car(s) being chased by other authorities, especially if we were working in and around the housing projects. The Los Angeles Housing Authority was on our tail on several occasions – especially in such posh complexes like Jordan Downs or Imperial Courts – but after our lights and sirens were activated, it usually backed off or aided in the traffic stop. Again, the adrenaline rush could not be matched.

After a while certain gangs got tired of running and merely complied with the shakedowns. One gang in particular, a Hispanic gang on the east side of the Newton area, always seemed to expect us. As a result, a mutual respect developed between the agents and the gangsters. One night we happened to jack this particular gang, and as we lined every gangbanger on his knees against a wall or fence, we noticed a new member who had joined the ranks. This kid was decked out in the normal gang attire: bandannas, saggy trousers, plaid shirt, and a bad attitude to go with it. However, this kid quickly lost the defiant countenance, possibly because he wasn't very good at acting like a shithead, possibly because he couldn't have been more than 11 or 12 years old! When one of our agents got around to interviewing the kid, he was asked what his street name was. The kid replied, "Gangsta Snail." This got a huge laugh out of everybody, including the other gangbangers. The kid was indeed a pre-teen and he soon became cordial, even thankful that he was being rousted by the cops, possibly for the first time.

We subsequently paid him back deferentially. From then on, any time we jacked this particular gang or one of its members, we always made a habit of asking for the whereabouts of Gangsta Snail. This kid became famous nearly overnight.

I don't remember ever running into him again, but when we made our subsequent swoops, we always made a habit of acting like we were looking for him to take him to jail. Being that it was usually one or two in the morning, odds are that Gangsta Snail was probably home in bed. Nevertheless, he became a local hero. I wonder what ever happened to him. . .

Though I never agreed with doing totally stupid shit, other agents most certainly did. This included kidnapping. There were two particular agents, who we called Frick and Frack*, who made a habit of it. They would jack a particular Crip or Blood gang and then subsequently handcuff one of the members to seemingly take him to jail. However, the route to the station usually took a different turn – the "scenic route" as we used to call it. And heavy metal interrogation techniques were the furthest thing from Frick and Frack's mind.

If the handcuffed gangster didn't cooperate (whatever *that* meant to Frick and Frack), the unlucky individual would then be dumped off in a rival gang's neighborhood and usually at two or three in the morning. Whether the gang member ever made it home is up for speculation, but it would seem doubtful being that any gangbanger in a rival's 'hood would surely not make it a city block before being confronted by the rival gang.

I never participated in this type of episode, but I never stopped it either. I just didn't want to know about it. Besides, I was new, and Frick and Frack were seasoned veterans. It was assumed that they knew what they were doing. Hopefully there was more "brag than fact" regarding this tactic, but either way it was another reason for gangbangers to fear us, and that was a good thing.

Jackin' was also a good way to work other areas of Los Angeles by getting out of the Newton precinct and its boundaries. If asked by our bosses why we had done an enforcement operation in another LAPD precinct, we would just say we had followed a vehicle away from Newton because it was obvious that it was up to something suspicious. The term "suspicious" was left to our imagination. We used to dub the subsequent pursuits as "Interstate Newton."

It also miraculously brought me back to the area of my old high school, which was in an LAPD precinct which bordered Newton. In the early 1980s, the high school was bordered on all sides by a series of gangs, groups who nearly a decade later would still control the same areas. The gang who used to shoot up my chemistry labs on a regular basis became our first and frequent target – with a vengeance! No quarter was given to these unfortunate souls. I won't give them any recognition here, but rest assured we fucked with them good. And often.

As stated earlier, the south side of my high school was bordered by a huge cemetery. One would think this was "dead" turf, but even this plot of land was controlled by a street gang, the Graveyard Boyz. These guys would always hang out outside the southern wall of the cemetery, and this proved to be a good location to congregate. Via street, there was only one way to approach these gangsters and it was from the south – about a quarter mile up a small hill from Washington Blvd. We didn't care if they saw us approaching or not, and usually when they saw a large sedan doing 80 miles-an-hour up this hill, the Graveyard Boyz were smart enough to know that whoever we were, we weren't there to pay respects to any deceased relatives. They – the Boyz, *not* the next of kin – would go barreling over the wall like Dwight Stones at Munich (remember him?) and would flee wherever they could. It became one of our nightly routines whenever we were ever in the area.

The Boyz also had decorated the southern walls of the cemetery with some highly artistic graffiti marking their turf (a common practice). We took many a photograph standing next to this wall, much as General Grant must have done after he took Vicksburg. It was all fun, though we were always ready to shoot it out.

One particular night we were "trolling" in the vicinity of my old high school. It was getting late (perhaps one or two in the morning), and my partners and I had decided to pack it in for the evening. But not without one final jack. We were all in one car, and as we drove south down Vermont Avenue I noticed a sedan ahead of us looking suspicious. By suspicious, I mean there were three to four assholes inside that didn't appear to be out to grab some late night take-out. I was in the back seat and I told the driver Chico* to pull the car over. As soon as Chico hit the lights and siren, the vehicle took off at breakneck speed. It was on!

We began the pursuit suddenly and it became the hairiest chase I would ever be a part of. The suspects drove maniacally. The car jumped center dividers, drove on sidewalks, and performed just about every moving violation possible. Thank God it was late at night and there were few cars on the road.

After nearly ten minutes (an eternity!) of white-knuckle fever, we finally got the sedan to turn down a dead-end street. As soon as the car came to the street's end, the driver stopped and bailed out of the car. There was a construction site in front of him enclosed by a chain-link fence nearly 30 feet tall; this didn't stop the runner, to our utter amazement. He scaled that fence in an instant and was gone. However, there were two other people who remained in the car.

As soon as we stopped behind them, these two gangbangers (who turned out to be teenagers) bailed out and tried to escape as well. (I address the Los Angeles Riots in a later chapter, but I just want to say that that night I learned what a car chase could do to one's adrenaline level.) As soon as we stopped, I jumped out with a shotgun and began chasing the two kids. There was nowhere for them to go, so we caught up to them swiftly. At that time I began kicking one of escapees in the ass; I don't know why I did it – it just came naturally. This became the only time in my entire career where I actually physically assaulted a suspect. As I continued kicking the teen, he kept yelling out, "Please mister, don't hurt me. I'm scared. I'm scared!"

I finally stopped my assault and flung the kid around and looked him in the eye. "You're fucking scared!?" I asked at the top of my voice. "What about me, you little fuck?!" I had completely lost it, but I did tell the truth; I was scared out of my wits.

We quickly handcuffed the two and began to search the car, and sure as hell there were two loaded handguns in the back seat. They could have opened fire on us at any time, but luckily for them, they didn't. Besides, we were ready. Since both suspects were young, we let them go. And, since it was late, we just took the contraband and split.

If one ever got bored or wondered where to find a good jackin' location, one needed to look no further than the local movie theatre. In the early 1990s, Hollywood put out a multitude of films documenting and glamorizing the gangster world and mentality. Pictures like *Boyz in the Hood*, *New Jack City*, and *American Me* made the rounds during this time, and as luck would have it, most of the folks who went to see these flicks were assholes themselves. Many cinema complexes experienced shootings, fights, and all sorts of revelry and "good times." We decided to have a look for ourselves.

I never paid to see one of these films, though some of them were quite entertaining. My usual vantage point was the parking lot outside the theatre. We usually let the gangsters watch the movie (no point in cheating the box office out of its take), but once the gangbangers left, they were all ours. I can't remember if we found a lot of contraband during these encounters, but I do know that *Boyz in the Hood* quickly became Boys *on* the hood. Once again, the gangbangers came to know who we were.

Another jackin' story came out of nowhere. Haley and I had gone to the gym in the late afternoon to get all pumped up because we were working that particular evening. On the way back to the office we noticed a car with two gangbangers cruising in front of us, and they didn't look like they were out for a leisurely drive in the ghetto. Haley, who was driving, decided to pull the car over. The only problem was I was dressed in gym attire, that is, dolphin shorts, a tank top, and tennis shoes. I did have my gunbelt though. So did Haley. He wore a similar outfit.

We buckled up our gunbelts and flipped the lights and siren to make the traffic stop. I didn't have a shotgun (a rarity), so my sidearm would have to do. I'll never forget walking up to the car and pulling the gangbangers out. They looked at us with lost eyes. They had no idea what was happening. One of the suspects asked me who we were with, and I replied, "the Fitness Police." That got a laugh from just about everyone. Haley and I handcuffed the two and subsequently tossed the vehicle. I think we found a little marijuana, but I just threw it in the gutter. I didn't feel like taking these guys to the city jail dressed like Richard Simmons. So, we let them go. Haley and I had a good laugh as we drove back to the office. I dubbed this incident as the "Post Work-out Shakedown." Pretty funny.

Lots of contraband was recovered during these impromptu raids. Knives were prevalent. After a while the gangbangers knew that it wasn't a good idea to have firearms on their persons, so knives became the likely alternative. For ATF agents, seizing knives during any enforcement operation wasn't in the manual. We could only, by law, seize guns, ammunition, and other federal contraband should it be so. Knives, at least to us, were not contraband *per se*, though they were weapons nonetheless. It's fair to say that over time we garnered a fairly large knife collection. We didn't throw them in dumpsters or return them to the gangsters because we knew they would always resurface – usually with a wounded or dead body attached. Instead, we just threw them all in a drawer at the gang task force office. We didn't do anything with them, just kept them off the street.

It's hard to gauge how many stabbings and/or murders we prevented, but I'm sure there were several. And we had everything: pocket knives, box-cutters, switchblades, and even some machetes. Nothing ever surprised me on the street.

The knife story had a peculiar ending. It just so happened that one tattletale agent called Internal Affairs on us after he/she found the cache in the desk at the task force. There's no way he/she could have found them without snooping, and as I had learned later about this person, he/she had made a habit of snooping in other agents' desks when no one was around. As a result Internal Affairs did come in and threatened suspensions for anyone involved with the procurement of the knives. One agent named Gilbert* took the fall for all of us and did a subsequent suspension for the drawer's contents.

As was almost never the case, Internal Affairs agreed with Gilbert's intentions (that is, getting the hardware off the street), but since the practice ran contrary to the ATF Directives, a suspension was handed down (though a relatively minor one). I'm forever grateful for Gilbert for being the fall guy (I had probably filled the drawer with the majority of blades). I'm also forever grateful for Gilbert for a host of other things – all commendable. Next to Haley, I probably learned more from him than any other. He was a stand-up guy and would take the fall for any fellow agent he knew was only doing his job. As for the tattletale agent, he/she faded away into leper obscurity.

Our task force also became a mini gangbanger clothing museum. In the early 1990s most gang members took pride in advertising their clique, and we had no problem in confiscating these items. When the gangsters put up a resistance, they were only told that they could be taken to jail under the "Anti Street Terrorism Act." I thought that had a nice ring to it. We collected gang hats, embroidered bandannas, jackets, even shoes from a multitude of gangs. No one ever asked where they came from, but if the question ever arose, we would just say the items were found on the street or abandoned in alleys.

I had jacked a particular gangbanger one afternoon who happened to be in possession of several marijuana cigarettes. I also noticed he had a finely-stitched leather belt that proclaimed the name of his gang. Instead of taking him to jail (he couldn't have been older than fifteen, and we didn't deal in juveniles), I made him a deal: I told him that since it was illegal for him to have the marijuana, then from that day forward he was to be my "friend." Instead of taking him to jail, I only told him that if he forfeited his belt, he wouldn't be dropped off with LAPD. Gladly the kid complied; he also became a very good informant over time, although I never formally documented him. [We as ATF agents couldn't use juvenile informants without parental consent (which would never happen); so we found other ways to utilize their services.] The belt was surrendered – I think we even returned the marijuana – and I wore that belt for many years. If anything I did that kid a favor, for I advertised his gang for a long time and in several states, though I don't think he ever saw it that way.

Over time jackin' became synonymous with the Los Angeles Field Division. Certain gang members even gave street names to several of us agents. It was all pretty hilarious. I had my own self-chosen moniker, Dr. Death. I had borrowed this alias from a defensive back who played for the Oakland Raiders during their heyday, and after a while my Ford

Mustang and I became a ghastly sight all over the Newton division, albeit not a welcome one to the many victimized gangbangers. Yet, a small amount of street cred(entail) arose between all parties involved.

Jackin' was definitely frowned upon by the brass, more so had they known the full extent of its usage. Yet, a time soon came where even jackin' became the accepted *modus operandi* of agents working south central Los Angeles.

This occurred in April 1992 after four LAPD officers were acquitted in state court for the much-publicized beating of Rodney King. After that date, all laws went out the window because Los Angeles had become an "official" war zone. During the ensuing days of civil unrest, many in the LA Field Division showed his/her true colors, mostly management, and SAC Sandoval more than anyone.

What happened among the LAFD brass during the LA Riots has remained an opaque and unspoken reality until now. I became disillusioned with much ATF did (or didn't do) over two decades, but it all began with the LA Riots. It became an unfair and badly-timed exercise in futility, lip service, and more shamefully, fingerpointing – something I learned over the years that the ATF higher-ups were astutely proficient in. It would begin in LA: it would surface again in Waco, Texas in 1993; resurface in Junction City, Kansas, in 1995; and, really rear its ugly head in Littleton, Colorado in 1999.

But for now, in April/May 1992, ground zero for the blame-game metamorphisized and metastasized in south central Los Angeles – all because of a righteous vehicle stop the previous year that tarnished the badge of every law enforcement officer in the country.

Chapter VI

Take Me To Your Leader

In south central Los Angeles each street and row of houses has an alley behind it. The original intention of city planners was for these alleyways to facilitate garbage pickup, emergency response, and other chores associated with civic maintenance.

What the founding fathers of LA could never have imagined was that these "thoroughfares" were to become Ground Zero of inner city crime. Granted, much overt crime occurred on front doorsteps, in the street, in cars, etc., but the truly entrepreneurial criminal did his work in these alleys.

As a result many became impassable – due to the intentional pileup of furniture or other garbage the denizens could get their hands on. We as ATF agents knew which alleys were "hot" as well as which ones were ambush zones. The Crips and Bloods had such ambush zones, but so did we.

Many times when riding in the 'hood late at night, I would wear a disguise, usually an ape mask. I'd had the costume for many years – brought out usually around the latter part of October – but I never could have imagined how perfect a disguise it would give me cruising the neighborhood.

As stated, I had a Ford Mustang 5.0 coupe that didn't look like a cop car, so I figured the added accoutrement of an ape mask would cement my presence in the 'hood as just another freak driving around looking for the shit. Anyway, I just wanted to fit in.

One late evening Haley came up with the uncanny idea of wearing night vision goggles (NVGs) while we did our police work in the alleys. Unlike the city streets which were lit (dimly at best), the passages behind the houses were pitch black and making out figures, animals, garbage – and other detritus that may have been lingering in these no-man's lands – was extremely difficult. So, Haley decided to test NVGs in this urban environment.

It seemed like a good idea.

If you've never seen NVGs, they were perfected by the US military, and ATF was lucky enough to receive several hand-me-downs for completely pitch-black conditions. The only drawback was you looked like an extraterrestial. The harness fit over the head quite nicely, and there were two three-inch lenses that protruded outward from in front of each eye. Each lens, when focused and coordinated with the other, provided a fairly good (though not perfect) view of what was in front of you.

I've since used NVGs in rural operations where the light of the moon was the only thing shining, but urban utilization proved to be the most memorable – and not for the reasons that could be imagined.

While seated in my 5.0. that night, I with the ape mask and a sawed-off shotgun between my legs, Haley began to affix the clumsy NVGs. We were parked right next to an alley that we were going to patrol. Both darked-out windows of my car were up as we prepared to do our thing.

While Haley was gearing up, I noticed a homeless and hopeless man begin walking towards the passenger side of my car. This guy could also have passed for someone or something from another world, but he had one thing in mind: getting a handout. As he approached the car I motioned to Haley, who had just completed donning his goggles. When the homeless man tapped on the passenger window, Haley wasted no time and let his window electrically go down.

At first there was one of those ear-deafening pauses, and as the vagrant slowly looked inside the car, my partner turned his gaze to meet our visitor. When the vagabond took one look at Haley, his eyes grew from marble size to cue-ball, and with that he turned around and did the fastest Jesse Owens impersonation I'd ever witnessed to get the hell outta Dodge! I'm not even sure if he saw me and the ape mask; the only thing he espied (and I'm sure never forgot) was the "alien" seated next to me who obviously had just landed in the 'hood from another solar system.

I've had to chase many perpetrators in my day, but I knew there was no way I ever could have caught that guy. All I could think about was what if the homeless had organized an Olympic relay team, they would have been untouchable.

And the last thing I remember is that those NVGs didn't work for shit in the 'hood. They just looked cool.

Chapter VII

The Los Angeles Riots of 1992

On March 3, 1991, or twenty years ago, the California Highway Patrol (CHP) began pursuing a car in excess of 100 miles-per-hour on a freeway in metropolitan Los Angeles. Three passengers were in the fleeing vehicle, including a man on felony parole named Rodney King.

The chase ran for many miles and finally ended in a residential neighborhood. CHP was able to arrest the two compliant passengers of the car, but the driver King refused to cooperate.

By this time, several Los Angeles Police Department crews had arrived to assist. King refused to submit and was subsequently beaten by the LAPD officers until subdued and finally arrested. The rest became infamous history.

It is not the purpose of these pages to pass judgment, give interpretation, or lay any blame on any of the participants. I wasn't there. However, having been involved in many high-speed chases, I do know this type of enforcement produces an incalculable adrenaline rush. Enough said.

Subsequently four LAPD officers were charged with excessive force for the King beating, but on April 29, 1992, after a seven-day jury deliberation, all were acquitted. What transpired afterward also became infamous history and ranks as the largest civil unrest episode in the United States in recent memory. To this day, the 1992 LA Riots rank alongside the Kent State murders, the 1968 Chicago Democratic National Convention, and ironically, the 1965 riots that also occurred in the City of Angels, as another shameful episode that demonstrates just how fragile our free society can be.

Regardless of the historical importance of April 29, the ATF agents of Los Angeles knew that their city had suddenly become an *overt* war zone. Up until that time we knew LA was a combat zone, but this fact was kept beneath the radar on many fronts. Now however, the war was out-in-the-open, just like the terrorist attack that would befall New York City in September 2001.

Our leaders, nonetheless, didn't see it that way, and how could they? They had never been on the front lines for the Battle of Los Angeles. We as the "grunt" agents had been, and we couldn't wait to get into action. Our federal bosses, however, wanted nothing to do with this seemingly *local* police problem.

The main political players in the riots, as it all played out, were LAPD Chief Darryl Gates, LA Mayor Tom Bradley, and subsequently California Governor Pete Wilson. ATF's chief player was SAC Lenny Sandoval who became the conduit between the LA Field Division and the upper echelons at ATF Headquarters in Washington DC.

As said, local agents were chomping at the bit to get involved. The verdict was handed down on Wednesday afternoon, and we as agents watched the city explode before our very eyes. We knew what had to be done.

As the stories of lootings began to circulate, we knew that there were many federal firearms licensees (FFL's) in south central Los Angeles that needed to be protected; if the looters had any mob-intellect whatsoever, those establishments would be the first to be hit. We also had informants from whom to glean critical intelligence should we be too late to save some FFL's.

Our leaders didn't see it that way.

To the astonishment of many, on the first day of unrest SAC Sandoval sent every agent home – only to remain on call (whatever that meant). This we accepted reluctantly, but since the civil unrest was still in its infant stage, a full realization and assessment of what was happening was still being analyzed.

However, Thursday, Day II, we received the same order from our superiors; agents were once again sent home; yet this time we were instructed to keep our pagers on and be ready for deployment (?). None of us understood what our bosses, especially Sandoval, were doing.

During these forty-eight hours I received countless telephone calls from LAPD officer friends of mine who told me that Chief Gates was asking for ATF help but was continuously given the runaround by ATF higher-ups, notably Sandoval. Even if Gates hadn't requested assistance, we still knew what had to be done and that we should have been out there on the front lines. I remember driving home that second day with firestorms burning all around me and wondering when we would get the call to engage. That call never came

Friday, Day III, ensued, and Governor Pete Wilson, after calling in the National Guard, also asked for federal assistance – this time formally. It would take the National Guard some time to arrive in Los Angeles from Central California.

As stated above, Chief Gates had been asking for federal assistance from the get-go, but the local ATF brass blew it off as only a *local* problem. By now the city was aflame (like Tokyo in a Godzilla movie) and nearly 5000 firearms had been looted and hit the streets. SAC Sandoval – obviously taking orders from back east – threw Chief Gates and Governor Wilson a bone by deciding to call out ATF SWAT teams from around the country who arrived over the weekend. These agents would subsequently accompany firefighters into the maelstrom to make sure no one was killed, but the damage had already been done.

Five thousand guns hit the streets as well as tons of ammunition. Fifty-three people had been killed, and over $1 billion in damage had occurred. Regarding firearms and ammunition, the local agents, given the blessing of our superiors (or even without it), could have at least prevented a large majority of this *targeted* looting.

SAC Sandoval however wanted no part of it. "No cowboys in my field division," suddenly took on the translation of "no sac on my person."

Soon and over the weekend, many of the "foreign" agents began arriving from all over the country, and not surprisingly, none of them knew the city of Los Angeles. The local agents' intelligence and knowledge of the city was an ace in the hole for SAC Sandoval, but he chose to ignore that as well.

By the time the weekend dawned, the fires were burning themselves out, but ATF was glamorlessly making its presence felt. For those of us who worked the city, it was an embarrassment. Not just to Chief Gates, whom we revered; not just to the LAPD, whom we idolized; not just to the Mayor, who knew his city was bordering on anarchy – but also to the countless, hapless citizens of south central Los Angeles who only wanted the mayhem to stop. These good people who happened to be at ground zero were the true victims.

ATF didn't give a shit about them, though many of the local agents did – myself included. I had several friends who lost their businesses in the chaos of those five days, and I never forgave my employer for facilitating its furor.

There was a disgusting denouement to all this, despite the fact that the four LAPD officers were subsequently retried and convicted, this time in Federal District Court on Civil Rights violations. As is usually the case with ATF, awards and commendations are given *ex post facto* when all the dust has settled and all crises have cooled off. The Los Angeles Riots were no exception.

Nearly every agent in the Los Angeles Field Division received a cash award for his/her efforts during the riots. Ironically, it was only taxpayer money being flushed down the toilet; ATF did absolutely nothing significant during this historic episode. What a shame!

We could have done a hell of a lot. And it wouldn't be the first or the last time. It was, however, a big lesson I learned: ATF was not in the habit of putting itself in harm's way – especially in situations that couldn't necessarily be completely gauged at the outset. ATF was also not in the habit of taking any chance that may have "besmirched the good name of the agency."

It wouldn't be long until I would see this demonstrated firsthand from my own ground zero.

Chapter VIII

Ghetto Crusader

I met a lot of idiotic people over the course of my career, but this guy ranks near the top. Pedro* and I were cruising the neighborhood one sunny afternoon in my Ford Mustang 5.0, when I noticed a small sedan in my rearview mirror that appeared to be following us. It was driven by a lone black male, and after observing him for several blocks I knew it was on. As stated earlier, my car had gotten me out of many tight spots, but this time I relished the occasion because we had this guy outnumbered and with faster wheels. Besides, I had a 12 gauge shotgun between my legs as did Pedro. So, the chase was on.

I quickly got on a major boulevard and headed north at about 90 miles per hour. I toyed with the sedan for a while, and it soon became apparent that its driver was having a difficult time keeping up with us. This was my cue to duck down a side street, flip a U-turn, and wait for my prey.

Whoever this person was (and we assumed it was a local gangbanger), he had now gone from hunter to hunted. As soon as I made a sharp right turn (nearly overturning my vehicle), I made a U-turn and parked in the middle of the street. Pedro and I in turn jumped out with our Remington 870 pumps and positioned ourselves behind the back of my car.

And, then we just waited.

It wasn't long before the silver sedan made the same turn, and upon seeing my vehicle, he soon slowed down to a near stop because he couldn't see us crouched behind the Mustang. As the sedan neared the back of my car the driver suddenly saw Pedro and I with guns leveled at his head.

He quickly hit the brakes, and before this guy could breathe I grabbed him through his window by the collar and jerked the guy out of the car and onto the ground. Pedro quickly slung his shotgun and handcuffed the individual as he cried for his life.

After the initial panic and adrenaline rush had lifted, we identified ourselves and asked the guy what the hell he was doing chasing us. He could only roll over to one side and utter the words, "I thought you guys were gang members! Please don't kill me."

Now, there were many times when I dressed the part while cruising the 'hood: bandanna, stocking cap, ape mask, whatever – but this was not one of those occasions. Pedro and I were probably the only two white males within a ten-mile radius. I asked the guy if we looked like gang members; he could only reply he wasn't sure.

He then began telling us that he had grown up in the neighborhood but had recently been discharged from the Marine Corps. I told him that was commendable, but was it a habit of his to chase every foreign car he saw cruising his street? He told us that he was sick of all the gang violence in his neighborhood, and he vowed to do something about it after he got out of the military.

We searched him and his car but found no firearms or other weapons. Not good to not bring a weapon to a gun fight. I also found a military identification card in this wallet which corroborated his story.

We removed the handcuffs and gave the guy some advice on how to stay alive, because the route he was currently taking would only result in him becoming a chalk outline on the sidewalk. He humbly concurred and thanked us for not shooting him.

ATF has a shooting policy granting an agent the right to shoot if a perpetrator is using his car as a weapon against the agent; so, this situation was a "gimmee" if I had really wanted to blow his head off. Again, my ATF training saved the day; many people would have shot in this scenario. I only held my ground, though I must admit my trigger finger was ready.

We schooled the guy and soon sent him on his way, but not after learning a lot about him and the neighborhood he lived in. He subsequently became one of my best informants, though his crusader days came to an abrupt halt that day.

Chapter IX

Exile Pt. I – Sent Out to Pasture

As I began working independently as an agent and also being assigned to the Newton Gang Task Force, I began to tally up a significant number of criminal investigations. There was one point where I carried approximately thirty open cases – a heavy load for anyone, especially a rookie. Moreover, the majority of these cases were very similar in nature, that is, gangbangers with guns and dope being charged with usually the same criminal violations. The search and arrest warrants were usually the same (with only a change of address and name of offender), and the spoils were almost always the same: firearms and crack cocaine. My bosses were very pleased with my work, but a time soon came when many of these cases began to go to trial – and all at the same time. I quickly found myself completely over my head. For some reason, preparing for trial – especially multiple litigations – was a subject not dealt with enough at the ATF Academy; so this was virgin territory.

Most of my defendants pled guilty to the main charges (or lesser offenses); so, preparing for a full-blown trial had never become an issue. That was before I began initiating prosecution on gangbangers who were looking at substantial sentences, including minimum/mandatory sentences.

It was around early 1992 that several of my cases were going to trial. Each case was handled by a separate Assistant United States Attorney (AUSA), but as I began dealing with the attorneys I began to question their methods. A big mistake.

I began receiving numerous calls daily about each case, including questions from the AUSAs that I deemed immaterial and unimportant. The AUSAs wanted to know everything about his/her case. For example, I was constantly asked who participated in the warrants; who found each particular item of evidence; who transported the prisoners to jail; was anything said by the suspects in transport, etc., etc. By this time every case looked the same, and I had great difficulty answering many of the queries put to me by the AUSAs. That was another mistake, and it was a genuine lesson I would learn from.

Truthfully, I could only answer the questions to the best of my recollection, but my memory was clouded by the simple fact that each case looked pretty much the same. We at the task force were executing as many as four search warrants a week, and I had no idea of the answers to these questions that came several months later as the cases approached their respective trial dates. Again, this was my oversight, and I would pay dearly for it.

I also learned at this time that the United States Attorney's Office (USAO) was not necessarily on our side, i.e., on the side of justice or on the side of the federal investigator. The USAO was a revolving door of attorneys who only wanted, for the most part, to be able to list "Federal Prosecutor" on his/her résumé before leaving to go into private practice.

I also learned that the USAO was a fraternity, that is, it was never wrong even when it was clear that it was. One example: I had loaned one AUSA a videotape taken of a warrant site we had hit. These videos were taken by us to preclude the residents from later saying we trashed their residence. We would film the house immediately after entry (to show what it looked like when we got there) and then we would film the place on our departure (to show how we had left the home – on many occasions in better shape than we had found it). The tapes weren't evidence by ATF policy, and were only taken as a prospective liability issue.

The USAO didn't see it that way, and rightfully so. Many of these videocassettes showed evidence in plain view, especially firearms, and this was best evidence for the subsequent prosecution of the case. Since ATF didn't mandate putting these tapes into property, we treated them as unimportant and only pertinent should a lawsuit emerge at a later date. Moreover, one tape could contain multiple warrant executions, and many of the cases that grew out from these enforcement operations were handled by different agents in the task force. In all, the tapes were just thrown in a drawer and forgotten about. Once I loaned a tape to an AUSA for his perusal, and it was subsequently lost by the AUSA, who later claimed to have never received it. This happened on more than one occasion.

Since we didn't treat the tapes as evidence, this was no big deal. However, it became a big deal later because the USAO did in fact say that these tapes were evidence and that we as agents were mishandling evidence.

I also met some interesting AUSAs while in Los Angeles – one in particular. Michael*, I found out, knew me from high school. Apparently he had coached a rival school's baseball team, and I had been the one on several occasions to sink his squad's hope of winning the league championship.

He was a semi-bigwig in the USAO and he called me into his office one day, and we reminisced about those high school days. I didn't remember him but I certainly remembered playing his team and beating them to win the league. He seemed cordial, and we just shared our memories, but I would soon learn that this guy had an agenda when I got into confrontation with some of the other AUSAs.

After some time, several of the attorneys began going to Michael (he was their boss) and complaining about the way I handled my cases and how I seemed to always be giving them the runaround. I did on occasion, but only because I failed to see the importance of the questions I was being asked. I had never had much regard for lawyers, and I let it be known to all of them when I thought I was being mistreated or condescendingly screwed with. That was yet another mistake.

Something I also didn't realize was that Michael wasn't the only one with an agenda; his bosses had one as well – and on a much grander scale. At the time ATF was flooding the USAO with all kinds of cases, and apparently the AUSAs were getting similar cold shoulders from many agents. This I would find out later. I, however, became a convenient fall guy.

The USAO was sick and tired of being shunned by us, and this presented itself as a fine opportunity to send an ultimatum to the ATF brass, most notably SAC Sandoval, that agents were not acting professionally and that the USAO wasn't going to take it.

Most SACs I have worked for over the years would have stood up to the USAO, but not Sandoval. He just cowered and bowed to the USAO's every demand. And its first demand was that it would not prosecute any case of which I was a part. In other words – based on my aloofness and seemingly uncooperative attitude – my days in Los Angeles were over.

My bosses met with Michael and other higher-ups in the USAO on a few occasions (all without me), and it soon became apparent that I was the sacrificial lamb. SAC Sandoval would eventually give in to all

USAO demands – the biggest one being I would have to be transferred out of the Central Judicial District of California. Sandoval would remind me (and others) on many occasions how single-handedly he had saved my job. That, I would find out, was complete and utter horseshit. He just didn't want to make any waves. Sound familiar?!

Back at ATF, Internal Affairs (IA) was called in to investigate each USAO allegation that I had mishandled cases, lied to AUSAs, and even allegations that evidence had been tampered with – an out and out lie. The "evidence" the USAO was referring to were the many videocassettes that we had taken at warrant sites. (To reiterate, these tapes, by ATF policy, were not evidence, and many were lost or misplaced. As stated, the USAO considered these tapes evidence; so, any misplacement or loss was considered sketchy at best in its opinion, if not an alright obstruction of justice.)

ATF would soon alter its policy after these events whereupon all warrant tapes were to be entered as evidence. It became known as "The Ging Memo."

According to the brass in Washington DC, this would be my only legacy to the Bureau after twenty years' service. This would become another lesson in the politics and smokescreen of ATF, that is, that ATF clearly didn't care how many people were put in jail by any one agent; what truly mattered to the higher-ups was that no negative "heat" should fall on the Bureau – from anywhere. Scapegoats and sacrificial lambs would have to pay for bringing such negativity on ATF. As will be seen, this truly manifested itself at Waco, Texas in the coming year, but I'll touch upon that travesty later.

For my "crimes," I eventually met with Internal Affairs for ten hours one evening. I soon learned that each player in this drama was interviewed before me, including each AUSA involved, and there were several.

I was basically interviewed last and had to answer for everything alleged. As a new agent with less than two years on the job I was scared shitless, to say the least. All I could do was tell the truth as I saw it. As I would learn later after several subsequent IA investigations (into me and other agents), IA really didn't care what the agent had to say, especially when it was the agent's word against a multitude of other people. Even if the agent was right and told the truth, he could still be suspended for "Embarrassing the Bureau, " – translation, bringing unwanted heat on the agency.

This charge was irrefutable in the eyes of the brass. I would receive many days "on the beach" over the years for violating this so-called *mantra of professionalism.*

In the above-described case, I would eventually receive a 45-day suspension without pay (later bumped down to thirty days though I never learned why) for mishandling cases and embarrassing the Bureau, though there was never any finding that evidence had been tampered with. Moreover, I was told that I would be transferred to another post of duty in which I would have no say.

At this point I didn't care; I was just happy to know I hadn't lost my career. I could only wait for that phone call from SAC Sandoval at a later date as to where I would be reassigned.

That call came nearly *a year later.*

In the interim I continued to work in the task force. I began to "ghost write" cases that other agents would take to federal court. In other words, I never slowed down, though I wouldn't be receiving credit for the criminals we were putting behind bars. I didn't care; the only thing that mattered to me was that these shitheads were going to jail.

On or around February 1993 I got the call from SAC Sandoval. I was driving southbound on Interstate 5 on my way to the office and I got a page from the SAC's extension. I quickly got off the freeway and called SAC Sandoval on his direct line. He was cordial and told me that I was being transferred to the Kansas City Field Division (KCFD), Denver I Post of Duty. At the time Colorado was part of the KCFD. SAC Sandoval told me that he had tried to get me transferred within California, but Denver became the most viable destination.

He told me that I would like it because Denver had its share of Crips, Bloods, and other gangbangers. That was cool, but I still sat at that payphone in complete shock. All along I had been told that I would probably be sent to San Diego, which was in a different federal judicial district. To this day I don't know if I was only told this to alleviate the embarrassment and pain of having to leave, but since it came from Sandoval I could only conclude that it was bullshit. Everything he said was.

My reporting date to Denver was June.

This move took an even greater toll personally, for at the time my marriage was on the rocks. When I got home that night and told my wife, she made it clear that she and my young son would not be going with me to Colorado. She wanted to stay in California. That was the ultimate suspension, but there was nothing I could do about it. ATF had never considered my personal affairs.

As I learned over the years, it never would. Nor anyone else's.

Chapter X

ATF Agent Drive-by: Act I

My first drive-by shooting occurred under unusual circumstances. First, I wasn't on duty; in fact, I had driven home from work early that evening to retrieve my personal car. (It was a major administrative no-no to use your government car for personal use, especially a night on the town.) Later that night I met up with some friends at a local tavern to have some pops and just reminisce. Somewhere between midnight and two a.m. I decided to drive home. A poor choice of course, but one I made nonetheless.

Unfortunately, I soon came up with other plans. For some reason my personal car never made it to my residence; instead, I wound up in the 'hood. I didn't point my car in that direction; I just wound up there – and at a familiar location.

At this time there was a neighborhood gang called the Dead End Boys*, so named because they controlled two four-story tenement homes that sat on a short cul-de-sac just off a major boulevard. These guys weren't the East Side Kids/Bowery Boys from the Hollywood films of the 1930s; these gangbangers were murderers and major assholes. I'd had several run-ins with them in the past and they definitely occupied an upper-tier position on my shit list.

The buildings were visible from the main avenue, and the Boyz, as we called them, had maniacal fun on occasion by shooting rounds at passing cars on this central thoroughfare. The police would sometimes respond, but by the time officers sifted through all the garbage and the hundred or so people that lived in these rat-infested structures, any crime scene had been wiped utterly clean. On occasion (as might be expected) the tenements also found themselves on the wrong end of the shooting gallery, and this night was one of those occasions .

As I neared the two buildings in my small little sedan I suddenly felt my rational self leave my physical body. It's hard to explain; to this day I have no idea why or what calling put me in that dangerous area that morning. As I drove slowly northbound on the main boulevard the buildings slowly came into view. Lights were on throughout, but for the most part the area was deserted.

As I got closer I could feel the hatred and rage welling up inside me. It took no thought whatsoever, though I had planned for leaving no evidence at the scene of the crime.

As I rolled by slowly I methodically removed my Smith & Wesson revolver and quickly squeezed off a full cylinder of rounds at the two establishments. I remember the muzzle flashes nearly setting my clothes on fire, but after all was said and done I was in the wind, not knowing if I had only hit stucco and wood or whether or not I had actually harmed a human being.

No spent casings were left at the scene, and as I sped away I soon realized that maybe I was no different than they. I had employed the same chickenshit tactics by indiscriminately spraying a faceless target; yet, deep down there was satisfaction, a downright glorification and delight that I competed on the same playing field as the Dead End Boys.

The sensation was fleeting, I must add, but I never felt overly ashamed or concerned for what I had done. In my mind the Boyz (and *all* street gangs for that matter) had declared war on everyone from the police to even their own peers. Well, so had I. This would forever become my mantra in the 'hood.

And after some time, even the gangbangers knew it.

ATF may never have made that much of a difference or dent in its crusade to clean up the streets, but we let it be known to the gangs that they had an even fiercer enemy than their rival gangsters.

It was the Feds, and they wanted no part of us.

Part Two

The thing that matters is not what *you bear but* how *you bear it.* -
Seneca

Chapter XI

Waco

I don't have a lot to say about the Waco tragedy, mainly because I wasn't there. Yet, sometime afterward, after I had been transferred to Denver, I was instructed by the Texas case agent to interview an eighteen year-old kid who lived in suburban Denver who had left the Mt. Carmel compound sometime in 1992; his mother had stayed behind and died in the conflagration that occurred in April 1993.

The interview questions were carefully scripted, so I knew I had to establish a good rapport with the kid from the outset; to be honest, I didn't know what to expect. As it turned out, rapport was easy, mainly because the teen was a guitar player as was I.

I don't remember the specifics of the interview but I do recall that the kid said one reason for leaving the compound was because David Koresh was indignant that the teenager could play guitar better than he. I could only shake my head in disbelief. If only the other eighty or so people had escaped because they could play a better guitar. Such runneth the blood of fanaticism.

As stated, I was not at Waco in February 1993 or anytime thereafter. I did, however, know many of the participants in the initial raid. Brave agents, all of them. One particular agent had been a past boss of mine and another was to be my future supervisor in Denver. Both were shot during the warrant execution, the former critically. Both lived, and I believe if they hadn't previously been in the military and in Vietnam, then neither would have lived.

ATF was not ready for any operation of this magnitude nor will it ever be. These two survived because they had been in such situations before; most of the participants had not, and it came into play that fateful morning.

I did not know any of the four agents who died that day in February, but I do know that they were heroic men whose names will be forever instilled in my heart.

What I know about Waco came afterward during all the subsequent investigations. I do know that the Branch Davidians knew ATF was coming that day, but that the ATF bosses ordered the assault anyway. I do know that afterward the entire country was looking to place blame for the debacle, and ATF initially tried to hand those in charge to the masses. This was a farce, for all these "leaders" were subsequently relieved of their duty though all were pensioned out and disappeared off the face of the earth. Yet, they'll have to answer for their idiocy at another time, and in a court they can't escape.

I also know that much blame subsequently filtered down to many of the street agents who had diligently worked the case, some in undercover roles. One of these agents, a friend of mine who I knew from Los Angeles, blew himself away in the office one afternoon with his duty firearm three years after the Waco affair. He never could get over the fact that ATF laid much of the blame at his footsteps, and as a result he took his own life. He also shot himself dead in front of another agent friend of mine.

It wouldn't be the first time a friend and coworker would take his own life, but I will deal with that subject later in this book, for it figures prominently in my own departure from the Bureau.

The big lesson I learned from Waco, besides all tactical lessons, was that the ATF higher-ups would cast anyone to the wolves in order to preserve the Bureau or their own careers. I had learned this firsthand in Los Angeles, but at least I still had a job. And my life. My friend in Los Angeles wasn't as fortunate.

I will never forgive the Bureau for that, but it was only the beginning.

Chapter XII

The Green Hornet

There was an agent in the Denver office, a good agent, who was soon transferred to another field division. He had a confidential informant who went by the moniker Green Hornet*. I had met the caped crusader before, and knew him to be smooth, but as I would later discover, he was also a major pain in the ass.

When the agent left on his transfer, GH was passed on to me as an informant. This guy could buy dope off the Pope, for he was that good. He was also in the habit of keeping a little pinch off the top for himself.

The first time I used him in a controlled buy he tried to pull this shit. I gave him $50 to buy crack cocaine from a dope house and he made the buy. He never left my sight and subsequently returned to my car with the purchased narcotics. We quickly left the area and drove to a staging location. I then frisked him (as I always did before and after the buy), and he then gave me the dope. Problem was, he gave me a baggie that only contained about $20 worth of crack.

I may have stated it before in another chapter: I was born at night, but not *last* night! I looked the Green Hornet in the eye and told him to fork over the rest of the crack. He finally relented and kind of laughed it off. I, however, didn't think it was funny. As I would soon find out, each dealing with him carried with it a thousand hours of drama, or maybe I should say half-a-ton of horseshit.

Over the ensuing months I would receive phone calls from him at all hours of the day and night. He always needed money or was in a bind, and I felt like he was using me as much as I was utilizing him. One day weeks later I decided to use him for another dope buy. The controlled purchase went like clockwork, but at the staging location afterward I quickly realized that he tried to rip me off again. This time I said nothing, but inside I had had enough of this asshole.

After my cover team left the staging locale, I decided to take the Green Hornet for a ride. I told him that I had my eyes on a location east of Denver that was supposedly selling drugs, and I asked him if he wouldn't mind going with me to check out the location. He agreed to come along.

Once you leave the metropolitan Denver area to the east, you are entering the farm belt of middle-America. This farmland stretches from eastern Colorado all the way to Indiana and is some of the richest farmland on the planet. It is also fairly deserted, and on that day that was a good thing.

We drove about thirty miles east of Denver, and I soon exited I-70 and began driving down a dirt road. There were no farmhouses in the area, only acres upon acres of farmland as far as the eye could espy. I soon pulled over to the side of the road and told the Green Hornet that I needed to take a piss. He did as well, and we both exited the vehicle. I never did unzip my fly, but GH soon took care of his business. When he turned around he couldn't believe what he saw.

I had unholstered my gun and quickly began firing rounds over his head. He quickly fell to the dirt and began crying out for his life. I only looked on with lifeless eyes and an even more sinister visage.

I quickly reholstered and told him to get to his feet. I then told him if he ever ripped me off again, I would kill him. I obviously didn't mean what I said, but that wasn't the point. The point was that I didn't like to be fucked with, especially by some two-bit street hustler. He got the message, got in the car, and I drove him back to Denver. I never used him again as an informant, though I did try to use his services on several occasions. He was nowhere to be found.

The Green Hornet had vanished off the face of the earth. I always treated my informants well, but I never hesitated to let them know who was in charge. Though the latter example may seem a little extreme, it did prove to be a good way of ridding myself of an asshole snitch. I couldn't have pulled that episode in Los Angeles, but maybe that was a good thing. Besides, I knew I would soon begin to like Colorado.

Chapter XIII

Club Fed

Nothing could have prepared me for Denver. I knew I would love the state, for I had always loved hiking and would soon get into snowboarding, rock climbing, and snow shoeing; yet, I was completely dumbfounded on learning the standard operating procedure of both Denver field offices. While in Los Angeles, each agent kept his government car armed to the teeth; all our cars contained shotguns, rifles, vests, and hundreds of rounds of ammunition; *that* way when we ever got called out, we had all our equipment with us. Denver was a little different.

Instead of having guns and ammo in the back of your car, each trunk now contained golf clubs, fishing poles, and racquet ball equipment. The two most important parts of the day were lunch and what activity one would be indulging in after work. This was a far cry from Los Angeles.

There were a few good agents in Denver, but I could count them on one hand. I also learned that the bosses in Denver didn't care much about production: you could produce no cases or compile twenty cases; each agent was treated the same and each received a great evaluation. The good agents were indignant about this, but expressing their opinions to the higher-ups did nothing.

We were the furthest outpost from Kansas City (our field division), and there was no leash on any agent prohibiting him/her from doing whatever he/she wanted. Some agents would go to movies during the day, hit golf balls, or go shopping.

Luckily, when I arrived in Denver I was able to quickly learn who was like me and who wasn't. After establishing myself somewhat I even had agents approach me and ask me to slow down because I was making them look bad. Some agents gave me hell for wanting to work nights and weekends. Well I didn't give two shits about this "advice," and I quickly told them to get out of my face. My overt indignations and swagger kept these slackers away from me.

One thing I learned off the bat was that Colorado was different from California in many respects. Soon after arriving in Denver, I assisted a search warrant execution in northeast Colorado. This was farm-belt country and tornado alley, I would soon discover. During the search of a barn on some farmland, we recovered bales of cultivated marijuana. I'd never seen so much "hippie lettuce."

Also recovered were some eagle or owl talons that hung from one of the barn's rafters. The Colorado Department of Wildlife was subsequently called in to make an assessment of the latter item. That assessment must have been quite damning, for I would soon learn about Colorado jurisprudence: the arrested subject received more jail time for the eagle claws than he did for the marijuana! I mean, he received something like five years for poaching. If he had stuffed the whole bird, he probably would have gotten the electric chair. I knew I wasn't in Los Angeles anymore.

In Denver I partnered up with a good agent named Brett*. Brett took me under his wing and introduced me to the Gang Unit of the Aurora Police Department (APD), a suburb of Denver. This unit resembled the Newton Gang Task Force, and I would do the bulk of my work with them. Unfortunately for me, Brett would soon be transferred out of Denver but not before he saw to it that I had partnered up with APD. We would do a lot of good work together that I will get to later.

I also partnered with another good agent named Ben Maxwell*. Ben had worked Denver his whole career, and I had briefly met him in Los Angeles when he came out there to look for a fugitive soon after the LA Riots. Ben was a ball-buster, and many of the other agents didn't like him because he was actually doing his job. Ben would subsequently introduce me to the Denver Police Department (DPD) Gang Unit, and this squad was another I would run with on occasion. In all, I wanted to continue working gangs, and Denver happened to be a good segue from Los Angeles. I even worked some of the same gangbangers I had worked in LA. Here's an example.

Soon after I arrived in Denver, in October 1993, two LAPD officer friends of mine were ambushed by gang members in the Newton precinct. Both were shot, one critically – though both lived. Miraculously they were still able to kill some of the attackers, though some escaped.

One gangster in particular, it was believed, had fled to the Denver area because he had ties there. I'm not sure how other big police departments do it, but when an officer of LAPD gets shot, the entire department circles its wagons and concentrates solely on finding the suspect(s). I'd seen this first hand in Los Angeles, but it was more than admirable that a day after this particular shooting, LAPD had detectives and Newton cops on a plane to Denver to hunt down the suspect.

One of the Newton Street officers was a friend of mine, and having come from LA, I devoted all my time to helping him and the detectives. To me, we were brothers.

Ben provided great assistance as well. In the course of a few days we turned the metropolitan Denver area upside down looking for this shithead. As it turned out, one of the people we contacted had been placing and receiving a disproportionate amount of phone calls (we subpoenaed the toll records) to a number in Hawthorne, California – a suburb of Los Angeles near LA International Airport.

This intelligence was quickly relayed to LAPD units who descended upon this two-story apartment one afternoon. I was not part of this operation, though it is worth relating.

As officers knocked at the front door of the residence, they saw an individual inside running towards the back of the apartment; radio traffic soon relayed this information. As other officers made their way around back of the complex, they witnessed the suspect jump off the two-story balcony and onto the ramp below leading to the underground parking garage. The leap was nearly a forty-foot launch!

The suspect quickly got up and ran, but not without firing a handgun at the pursuing officers. It didn't take long for the cops to shoot the assailant, and after dumping him and seeing his pistol go flying, it appeared that the search and pursuit were over. They couldn't have been more wrong.

The gangbanger quickly got to his feet and began running again; moreover, he pulled another pistol out of his jacket and began shooting again at the officers. His luck soon ran out however when he ran towards a tree where a Newton cop, another friend of mine, was hiding with a shotgun. One blast and the gangbanger was toast. He was indeed the person LAPD had been looking for, and it was now over, but most were in disbelief because – as was learned later – this guy had been running down the street with two severely broken ankles sustained after jumping off the balcony.

Another lesson learned: don't ever discredit the rush of adrenaline.

I remember hearing the news back in Denver of the outcome, and I felt extremely proud that I had been able to assist my LAPD brethren.

Ben had also been a tremendous help, for at the time I was still learning the city. Ben's geographic knowledge saved us countless hours.

He and I would soon receive commendations from LAPD, and to this day it stands as one of my finest achievements as a law enforcement officer. ATF, on the other hand, didn't even give Ben and I a high-five. As I would learn later, it rarely did.

While other agents were busy playing computer poker or shopping over-the-phone at the office (this was before the internet), Ben and I hit the streets hard. In 1994 Congress had passed the Brady Bill, legislation that required gun purchasers to undergo a criminal background check before they could take possession of the weapon(s). This precluded many ex-cons from simply going into a gun store, falsely filling out the paperwork, and exiting the business with their firearms. Now the *modus operandi* got a little more interesting – and dangerous. Denver, as well as other cities, soon saw a dramatic spike in gun store robberies and burglaries – many of which involved store employees being killed and/or injured.

Ben and I, along with the local gang units, soon began concentrating on these types of cases. And, we were very successful. Ben and I became the gun store theft gurus. I can't remember how many we solved, but we sent countless gangbangers to prison for those crimes. And yes, they were being committed by street gangs. One such case is worth talking about.

Dave's Guns was a federal firearms licensee (FFL) in metropolitan Denver and was perhaps the largest and most well-known FFL in the city. Moreover, Dave, the owner, was a good friend of Ben's as well as a friend to most law enforcement officers in town, for Dave's main customers were cops. Dave's Guns mostly carried high-end firearms, and the business was extremely well-run. It would take a very audacious cat to walk into this place and pull a robbery or burglary (for all employees were well-armed), but that's just what happened late one night after closing.

Several hours after the place has closed, three gangbangers managed to break into the business through the ceiling, and before the police could arrive they had stolen more than forty firearms – handguns and rifles. These guns would soon hit the street, and this is where Ben and I began our manhunt.

It didn't take long to run down the people responsible for the burglary. I can't remember exactly our first big break in the investigation, but I believe it occurred when a certain gangbanger was arrested with one of the stolen handguns in his possession. As it turned out, this guy had been one of the three burglars. We put the screws to him pretty hard, and it wasn't long after that we began looking for the other two perpetrators.

The arrest of the latter two nearly involved a full-blown shootout during a traffic stop by Aurora PD, but the two gangsters thought better. They were captured with some of the stolen firearms as well as a significant amount of crack cocaine.

But the case didn't end there.

Follow-up investigation led to the arrest of five additional people who had received some of the stolen firearms or had been accomplices after the fact. All eight went to federal prison. One of the after-the-fact suspects pled guilty to trading an ounce of crack cocaine for some of the firearms. Our case against him was weak at best, for we had no dope evidence or any of the bartered firearms. Nevertheless, this idiot pled to the charges and was shipped off to the real Club Fed – the penitentiary.

Years later, after he had been released, I ran into this guy in a Hooter's restaurant. We, of course knew each other. I was with my girlfriend at the time and didn't want to start any trouble, but I let it be known through my eyes to this guy, that if he wanted some trouble, then I would oblige him. I'm sure he had a firearm, and the fight would have been somewhat one-sided because I was unarmed. But he knew better. He and his buddies would soon leave and I would never see them again.

Denver wasn't and isn't that big of a town; I would run into several of my arrestees over the years, but no trouble ever ensued. I always knew my place but would back down to no one.

As stated above, I began working many gangs and gang members who I had known or knew from my LA days. One particular guy's arrest is an amusing story.

I had heard of him in LA, and he went by the moniker of T-Bone*. T-Bone was a Newton Precinct gangster who had relocated to Denver to make his fortune in the illicit gun and crack cocaine trade. He had recently been picked up by the Aurora PD for drug and gun possession, but was looking at very little time in state prison, if any. I decided to pick the case up and take it federally because I knew he'd get more time. I was able to get a federal arrest warrant, and after we found out where he lived, we decided to do some surveillance in and around his residence.

T-Bone was staying in an apartment complex in east Aurora. Most of Aurora is surrounded by farmland, and this complex was no exception. There was an irrigation canal on the east side of the apartments adjacent some trees, and I knew when we finally made the arrest it would be a good place for a sniper to hide and perhaps engage should T-Bone try to escape. The irrigation ditch was dry, and it would be an easy place for the sniper to set up. That sniper would be me.

Come the day of the arrest, Aurora PD officers and I established ourselves around the complex and waited for T-Bone to get in his car and drive away. The plan was as soon as he started to drive away from the apartments, two APD cruisers would box him in and make the arrest. Moreover, from my sniper position I would be directly across from T-Bone's driver's side door, precluding any crossfire issues.

It was after dawn that we established our positions, though I remained in my car on the east side of the complex. We had positioned a van in the parking lot directly across from T-Bone's front door, and when the radio call came out that he was getting ready to get in his car and leave, I quickly exited my car and headed to my position with my Colt AR-15 rifle. There was one thing, however, I hadn't counted on.

When I got to the irrigation canal, I found it full of water! I was short on time and knew I would have to cross the stream to get to the tree that was to be my sniping position. I was shit-outta-luck, as they say.

I then raised the rifle above my head and began fording this mini river. The water came up to my chest, but since my adrenaline was flowing I thought nothing of it. And it was winter! I soon got to my position and waited for T-Bone.

The plan worked like clockwork, and as soon as the APD cruisers boxed him in, he was directly in my line of fire. I could tell that he thought about running the roadblock (or exiting the car and fleeing on foot), but when he turned to his left and saw me and my rifle pointed straight at his head, his eyes grew to the size of basketballs. He surrendered without a fight and was taken into custody.

As my adrenaline soon subsided, I began to get cold, but everyone present got a good laugh at the federal agent who had to cross the freezing moat to get to his destination. Anything for the catch, right!?

Another good case of mine also began in Los Angeles. A friend and ATF agent there called me one afternoon and said that he was working a methamphetamine dealer in San Fernando (an LA suburb) who was tied to a firearms and explosives guy in Aurora. I soon began working the Colorado side of the case, and the investigation grew exponentially, encompassing four states and nearly ten defendants.

The first encounter began in a Los Angeles hotel room – surreptitiously wired-up by our tech guys – where a pound of meth was traded for a machinegun. An informant for the agents in LA had done a controlled purchase earlier in the day, and that night that pound of meth was traded for a machinegun provided by the bad guy.

Though it never became an issue later – which stunned everyone who worked the case (except, thankfully, the judge) – we had let this pound of drugs just go back on the street. It turned out to be a good move, however.

Soon the LA agents began making contact with the source of the machinegun who lived in Aurora, Colorado. This individual and an accomplice could also procure explosives, specifically pipe bombs.

Subsequently a deal was set between undercover agents and the criminals behind an outlet mall in Castle Rock, Colorado.

It was a huge undertaking; anything that involved explosives was. We positioned multiple snipers on the roofs, had agents hiding in dumpsters, and basically had the entire area under our control. The exchange of methamphetamine for pipe bombs was scheduled to take place behind the mall at 2 A.M., precluding the chance of any civilians being injured or killed should the bombs detonate. (Contrary to the belief of many, with us civilian safety always came first.)

The undercover agents first met the suspects in front of a motel down the interstate, and the whole party soon drove north to the rear of the mall. The crooks had never met the undercover agents in person; they had only spoken over the phone (all calls of which were recorded). The crooks didn't think it was strange to travel to an unknown location to do the swap (I sure as hell would have!), and the operation went like clockwork.

One of the undercover agents gave a prearranged signal for the arrest team to move in, and the capture happened without incident. The case would also yield additional suspects who had participated in the pipe bomb construction, and as stated, nine or ten people went to federal prison.

Two of the crooks received life in prison without parole. It was the biggest hit I ever had in terms of sentencing, and overall the case was worked flawlessly by everyone involved – a *rare* occurrence.

As stated, Colorado was not California. And this applied to the judges as well. I remember I had a case on a guy, a convicted felon, who kept pawning a pistol at a local pawn shop whenever he needed the cash. Each time he pawned the gun, a new charge would be tallied. I just let him go and go for several months before I finally decided to arrest him.

The arrest was pretty funny. It was winter and cold, and we had several ATF cars watching the house. We didn't know if the suspect was inside, and with an Arrest Warrant, you couldn't just walk up and bash down the door until you were absolutely sure your suspect was inside. Unfortunately my Domino's Pizza trick wouldn't do much good at six in the morning. So, I came up with another ruse.

Somehow I had gotten the guy's phone number, and I placed a call that frigid morning around daybreak. After I dialed, a male answered the phone. I asked for James Fields*. I was told that I was talking to him. I then said I was so-and-so from K-whatever radio station, and he, James Fields, had just won concert tickets to the Butthole Surfers. For some reason that was the only band I could think of – probably because I was going to their show in a few weeks. Brett was sitting next to me and laughing his ass off. Well, Fields acted all happy, and I told him that the tickets to the show would be sent to his house in the coming days. He was stoked. He was a big dude, too. He looked like James Hetfield of Metallica. Thus, the reason I had ten agents out on the arrest. We subsequently entered the home without incident, hooked the guy, and took him to federal court.

As the case progressed I began to learn a lot about Fields. He had a job (most of my perps didn't), he had a family, and he was only putting the gun in-and-out of pawn to pay bills. So, I went to the Assistant United States Attorney (AUSA) assigned to the case and told him to recommend probation for the guy, if not drop the case altogether. Fields was just trying to support his family. The AUSA agreed, and he recommended to the court that Fields receive only probation.

Well, the judge didn't see it that way.

His Honor, District Court Judge Edward Nottingham of the Judicial District of Colorado, was known as a "hanging judge," but I didn't see it firsthand until the Fields case. He had been appointed by President George H.W. Bush in 1989, and I soon discovered why Bush liked this guy. Even though we, as the prosecution, recommended probation for Fields, the "Sheriff of Nottingham" (as he was called by just about everyone) gave Fields three years in federal prison! I sat in the back of the courtroom and watched in utter shock and watched Field's wife and children crying uncontrollably. I felt like such an asshole. No angel, that's for sure. That was the last time I ever did a case like that, and it hurts me to this day.

I also developed a great working relationship with other federal agencies in Colorado, notably, the Drug Enforcement Administration (DEA). I hadn't done much work with DEA in Los Angeles, though we did have a metropolitan group that teamed with DEA. My first encounter with them occurred in Colorado during the aforementioned eagle talon caper. Every Colorado DEA agent was first-rate, many reminding me of my ATF cohorts back in LA. After a while I would get called all the time by friend DEA agents who were getting ready to execute a search warrant. I was always asked if I would like to come along, and I never passed up a chance, for there were always guns to be found.

One warrant execution I remember vividly. It was late one afternoon when I got a call from a pal DEA agent who told me that they were going to execute a search warrant later that night in a northern suburb of Denver. The suspect was a twenty-four year-old drug trafficker who lived with his wife and young daughter. He was also a man, allegedly, who was known to like his guns.

The house was a two-story family home in a nice neighborhood (something I wasn't used to) , and he indeed had all the toys. He had fast cars, a boat, jet skis, Harley Davidson motorcycles, everything. And, man oh man, did he like his guns!

He had over a hundred firearms, high-dollar shit, including a fully-loaded machinegun which sat next to the front door. Thank God the guy wasn't there when we hit the place. I never considered the suspect the best father figure either, for under his daughter's mattress were a dozen assault rifles! (A little aside: his wife would serve him with divorce papers the day of his Initial Appearance in Federal Court – I guess she didn't think he was the greatest dad either.)

I would come to learn that night what it was like to have broad seizure authority. At ATF, we could basically only seize as property firearms and ammunition. We could only seize a car if it had moonshine in it, or a machinegun, or a bomb. For the most part, every chance I had to seize a vehicle went down the toilet, because the vehicle in question was more-than-likely a piece of shit.

The DEA had a much broader seizure authority, and they went after some high rollers. If the DEA could prove that items such as cars, boats, planes, etc., were purchased with drug money, then all those items could be seized.

That night in north Denver soon became a scene out of *The Grinch Who Stole Christmas*. The DEA agents took everything. Each agent drove an SUV with a trailer hitch, and since the suspect had his motorcycles, jet skis, and boat on trailers in or around his garage, the DEA agents just hooked up the trailers to their cars and took the booty to their office.

The seized cars were just driven back to the office by agents who hadn't brought their own vehicles to the warrant execution. They even took the house! Like the Grinch, they didn't leave a thing. It was awesome.

I, unfortunately, got to take the guns – paperwork of which kept me busy for many days. I had heard stories in the past where DEA had seized more in assets from criminals (i.e., in absolute dollars) than it had received in its budget from Congress. This was the Major Leagues. ATF wasn't even Rookie Ball, for those who know the minor league system. DEA was the shit!

Such was some of the work in Colorado. It took some time to establish myself there, but soon I was working at a good clip. I was still disillusioned with many of the Denver agents, but by this time it didn't really matter because I had other people I could work with. I would also learn a lot about my co-workers priorities when a coworker, an agent in Colorado Springs, was shot by gang members on a drug deal gone bad. The agent who was shot had been stationed in Denver when I had been transferred there, but he subsequently received a transfer to the Colorado Springs field office. This office, I would learn, was in complete contrast to the Denver offices, and it reminded me of the field offices in Los Angeles. This office wanted to work.

Each agent was a go-getter, the boss was first-rate, and the criminals were scared of these guys.

However, one afternoon during a meeting of crooks and an undercover agent, one of the criminals pulled out a gun and shot the undercover. The agent Craig* was a good friend of mine, and thankfully he didn't sustain any life-threatening wounds. The shooter, however, escaped but not after a pretty eventful shootout whereupon he too, it was believed, had sustained a bullet wound.

I was in the Denver I office that afternoon though most of my co-workers had gone home for the day. I received the call from Colorado Springs, and as soon as I hung up and notified every other Denver agent, Ben and I were speeding down I-25 at 100 miles-per-hour to lend our assistance. Strangely, we were the only agents in Denver to immediately respond and without thought. It would be hours before any other Denver agent arrived to help out, obviously after the bosses had ordered them to get there asses down there.

Ben and I, along with the Colorado Springs agents, turned the city upside-down looking for the shooter; we had all hospitals on alert as well as all transportation centers, but it was later learned that the suspect had escaped somehow and gone to Los Angeles.

This was good news to Ben and I but bad news for the suspect, for I knew if anyone in the country could find this asshole, it was my brethren in LA. He indeed was found by the LA agents and arrested without incident in San Pedro, California. And sure as hell, he had taken a bullet in his leg.

The Colorado Springs agents didn't much like or respect the Denver agents (rightfully so), but they would never forget how quick Ben and I had responded and offered our assistance.

I became great friends with all the agents down there, for they reminded me of my compatriots back home in LA. In the years that followed I would assist them any time they asked for my help, which was frequently. I wanted to be transferred there, but the bosses would have nothing of it. Why should they? I, along with a few other agents in Denver, was making them look good. They weren't about to let me go.

I also learned that there were some agents who wouldn't even do their job when out on an enforcement operation. The following story I'll never forget, for I thought Ben Maxwell was going to kill a fellow agent.

Ben and I had gotten a search warrant for a farmhouse in Erie, Colorado, which is about 30 miles north of downtown Denver. I don't remember anything about the warrant or the suspect, but I do recall that we found a boatload of evidence – most of which was stolen property. This guy had stolen motorcycles, cars, and even a Caterpillar front-end loader that must have cost over $150,000. We had to call in a forty-foot semi tractor-trailer to haul all the vehicles away. The Caterpillar rip-off had to have taken some balls; even I was impressed.

In the house we found an indoor marijuana grow, multiple firearms, and thousands of rounds of ammunition. The warrant site covered many acres and contraband was found all over the property. Adjacent the main house, perhaps fifty yards from the front door, sat a single-wide trailer which served as a kind of guest house. Making entry into the trailer was fairly comical because I banged on the front door with a battering ram for many minutes to no avail. Had anyone been inside with an axe to grind (or a trigger to pull), then I would have been a dead man. The lesson learned here was to always have a contingency plan for another point of entry. Had I merely walked around to the other side of the trailer, I could have just walked in, for the back door was open. Oh well.

Once secured, several agents were instructed to search the trailer while the rest of us, Ben and I included, oversaw the search of the main house, which was loaded with contraband. Several hours after being at the site, several Denver agents were growing restless because they wanted to leave and get back downtown (or home). I wanted to get the hell out of there too, but we had to wait for the tractor-trailer to arrive.

After the main house had been thoroughly searched, Ben and I decided to go have a look in the trailer. The agent put in charge of the latter search told us that no evidence had been found inside, but Ben and I decided to have a look anyway. Another lesson: just because one agent doesn't find any evidence does not mean that another agent won't find something. Yet, one would have had to be blind not to recover what we found.

Ben and I found guns in plain view, marijuana in an uncovered serving bowl in the freezer, and a host of other illegal items. I was pissed off to say the least, but Ben completely flipped his lid! And rightfully so.

He vehemently confronted the other agent, and had our supervisor not been there to break it up, there probably would have been a gun battle. I would have let it happen.

The agent in question was a renowned slacker, so it was partially my fault for letting him lead the search of the trailer. Another lesson: don't bring slackers to the big dance.

Speaking of slackers, it was in Denver where I had my first brush with ATF Regional Counsel – or maybe I should say brush-*off*. ATF keeps on its payroll a horde of attorneys to deal with all sorts of cases and issues relating to the federal firearms and explosive industries. Since ATF licenses dealers in guns, explosives, tobacco, and alcohol – there is a need to have on hand a legal team to deal with some of the biggest manufacturers in the nation.

These retained attorneys would also assist agents in their cases should the case agent need some type of legal advice. I had always found Regional Counsel helpful when I had a question, but when it came to seizures, the pool became a little more opaque.

I remember one attorney, Joshua Rosen-Rosen*, who was the Regional Counsel for the ATF Phoenix Field Division. (The Denver offices were transferred to the Phoenix Division in 1997.) I had a particular case in Colorado where I was trying to seize over 100 firearms from a convicted felon who worked at a gun store. It was a family-run business, so I figured I could take the guns because one of the family members, a clerk in the store, was a convicted felon and major pain in the ass for local citizens and law enforcement.

Rosen-Rosen, who I will call R^2, was assigned the case because the family contested the seizure. This thing dragged on and on. I kept trying to get R^2 to give a ruling, but he only let the case drag on and on and on. I would call him constantly but would not hear from him.

This went on for over a year. Finally, I said, "Fuck it." I gave the guns back. Since they weren't street-type guns, I had no problem returning them. The paperwork to do so was a nightmare, however.

I would never forget the treatment I got from R^2, but this was Regional Counsel in a bottle – they were worthless. Coincidentally, R^2 and I would cross paths several years later in Phoenix.

It was also while stationed in Denver that I got my first glimpse at how ATF liked to piss away taxpayer money. In August 1998, I was asked to assist some Cheyenne (WY) agents who had an operation going in Hulett, Wyoming, in conjunction with the annual biker run just over the South Dakota border in Sturgis. It was intended to be an intelligence gathering mission, but as I would soon discover, it was only a way for one Cheyenne agent, with Phoenix Division approval, to take a week-long vacation in northern Wyoming.

The original "mission" was to gather information and take pictures of any outlaw bikers who happened to attend the annual Sturgis motorcycle run. What I didn't know was that during that first week of August, Sturgis had more cops per capita than any other city on the face of the earth. Any outlaw biker with half a brain wouldn't venture within the city limits without being rousted by the local cops. So, these "outlaws" only stayed out of town at a few campsites, which were basically off-limits to the police. If any criminal activity occurred at these camps, the police didn't really give a shit because it was outside of town.

The agent from Cheyenne didn't care about anything it seemed; he just wanted to have a good time. And as a result thousands of taxpayer dollars were flushed down the toilet during this operation.

My only duty during the week was to walk around town and get drunk, in other words, to just fit in. I did meet some new friends – one new ATF agent who would factor later in my career in a huge way – but for the most part Sturgis was just one big party. And, an expensive one, for no intelligence came out of this operation. We did snap some interesting photographs however.

Over the years – and this is something I'm ashamed of – I even began to become like the other Denver agents, at least at times. There were times when I'd tell my boss I was working up in a county in the mountains, when in reality I'd be snowboarding. Sometimes I would tell my supervisor I was procuring records or doing surveillance in Boulder County; this surveillance was actually me rock-climbing in the Flatirons, a world-famous city park and rock-climbing mecca near the University of Colorado. If ever called on the carpet, I could always say I was participating in physical fitness, which agents were paid four hours a week to take.

I was always in shape (I had won the Physical Fitness Award at the ATF Academy), so there was never any doubt I was using those four hours to good end each week.

However, if something arose on the job, then physical fitness got shelved. Not so with other agents and staff members; they were religious in making sure they used those four hours every week. Many questioned the results, for many of these "religious types" were grossly out of shape, overweight, and basically useless. Still, nothing was ever done about this.

Such is the ATF way.

Chapter XIV

Adopt A Highway

I was relatively new to the Denver I Field Office, and word soon came down that the Kansas City Field Division would be holding an all-hands conference in Kansas City for every agent in the field division. The KCFD comprised Colorado, Missouri, Kansas, and Nebraska; so, this was to be the hayseed party of all parties. Due to budget constraints (or so we were told), the Colorado agents had to drive to Kansas City. As a result, two of my new compatriots and I set out on a Sunday morning in route to the barbeque capital of the world; the conference was scheduled to begin on Monday.

These types of "all-hands meetings" usually coincided with the end of the fiscal year (i.e., September), when there was money that had to be spent, and such gatherings were always a good way to exhaust the "kitty." ATF is renowned for holding "conferences" when there is money that has to be spent.

The three of us left Denver early on Sunday morning (it was a 600 mile drive), and things were about as uneventful as one could imagine driving across the heartland of America. However, it wasn't long before the boredom was soon interrupted.

Anyone who has driven cross-country is familiar with the "Adopt A Highway" campaign. Local people, or certain organizations, have their name on a sign on the Interstate basically saying that all litter for the next mile or two is policed and thrown away by the aforementioned sponsoring organization. Signs usually read, "The 4-H Club of whatever town" or "the VFW or American Legion of said county." This day would always be remembered.

As we were driving in the vicinity of Salina, Kansas, on Interstate 70, one of the Adopt-A-Highway signs popped up: it read, "This particular leg of I-70 is policed of all litter by the N.A.A.C.P. of Salina, Kansas." Suddenly the car went silent. The radio was turned off and all cigarettes extinguished. At the time I was in the back seat of the vehicle reading a book. My two officemates were in the front seats. The driver, who smoked about a pack of cigarettes every 200 miles, just grinned and electronically rolled down all the windows.

Not a word was said, but as soon as we passed that NAACP sign everything that wasn't nailed down in that car went out the window: the voluminous Sunday papers, beer cans, cigarette butts, road maps, everything.

I didn't say a word and only played along, but I knew if my Los Angeles brothers (not to mention anyone else) could have seen this, then there would have been hell to pay. Later I felt ashamed because I did nothing about it; I even threw trash out of the window so as not to ruin the "show." I knew at that moment I had come a long way from Los Angeles, and from that day forward I could only hope that I could get back and escape this freakshow.

It was a feeble hope. Not only that – I had ignominiously become part of the circus.

Chapter XV

The Oklahoma City Bombing

On Wednesday April 19, 1995, at approximately 9 A.M. CDT, the Alfred P. Murrah Federal Building in Oklahoma City was destroyed by explosives, leaving 168 dead – including nearly 20 children – and nearly 700 injured. Prior to September 11, 2001, it was the worst terrorist attack to ever occur on American soil. Soon after the detonation, soon-to-be suspect Timothy McVeigh was pulled over by an Oklahoma State Trooper for having no license plate on his vehicle and for carrying a concealed weapon. The magnitude of this seemingly unrelated traffic-stop would soon unfold.

In the ensuing days it was learned that the bulk of the crime's planning and preparation had happened in and around Ft. Riley, a huge army base located in Junction City, Kansas – approximately 65 miles west of Topeka and 270 miles north of OKC. To give you an idea of the size of Ft. Riley, it is located in two counties, covers more than 100,000 acres and is home to nearly 30,000 people. It is also the home of the 1st Infantry Division of *Big Red One* fame. This area became the true ground zero of the crime, at least in terms of preparation.

As agents stationed in Denver, we knew we were going to be detailed to Junction City; in fact, Ben Maxwell and I were chomping at the bit to go. Other agents, we soon discovered weren't so eager. That didn't matter, for every Denver agent was told to pack a bag for at least a month and report to Ft. Riley as soon as possible.

Riley sat 475 miles from Denver, so the commute would take some time; other agents from around the Kansas City Field Division would also respond, but we had one of the longest commutes. Considering the historical importance of this assignment, Ben and I wouldn't have cared if we had to drive to Nome, Alaska. We partnered up and arrived in Junction City the ensuing weekend.

A command post was set up on the grounds of Ft. Riley and heavily guarded by sentries, concentina wire, armored personnel carriers, and sandbags. No one was getting into this place without the proper credentials, and that was fine with us. The FBI was running the overall investigation and its off-shoots, but it welcomed all the help from other agencies, federal, state and local.

I had always had my suspicions about the "Feebs," as we called them, but over the ensuing weeks my respect for this agency became immeasurable. We were always treated as equals, and if we needed anything, it would be procured. I became amazed at how the FBI conducted itself; its seemingly endless resources; its access to anything and everyone; and, its overall swagger. In all, it put ATF to shame, and this would highlight itself even more in the coming weeks.

As investigators began arriving at Ft. Riley from all over the country, the multitude was soon divided up into squads. Each squad contained various FBI agents and other federal and state law enforcement officers, and each had a specific function. For example, one squad would solely be assigned the task of dealing with the Ryder truck used in the bombing; another with McVeigh; another with Terry Nichols (who was soon identified as one of McVeigh's accomplices); and, others with finding out where the suspects had procured the explosives.

Ben and I were assigned to the squad that had the sole duty of finding out where the suspects had procured the ammonium nitrate fertilizer used in the blast. Ammonium nitrate (NH_4NO_3) is a white crystalline solid made up of "prills", very small beads/balls about the size of a grain of sand one might encounter on a Florida beach. It is rich in nitrogen, and thus is used as a popular fertilizer. It can also be used as an oxidizing agent in explosives, and as intelligence began arriving from OKC, it was determined that ammonium nitrate had been used in the blast, based on the number of unconsumed prills that littered the blast scene. Putting two and two together, it became likely that McVeigh and Nichols had probably procured the ammonium nitrate somewhere in Kansas.

It became my squad's principal duty to find out where. Since its common use was that of fertilizer, we dubbed our unit the "Shit Squad."

Being that Kansas is located in the Farm Belt, this job was not as simple as it may sound – despite the amounts that had been procured for the bomb. Every town and grain silo in Kansas sold ammonium nitrate; so, our instructions were to go to every town in Kansas if need be to find out if a large amount of this stuff had ever been purchased and/or stolen. It was a tall task, but one we welcomed.

A typical day in the day of the OKBOMB task force, of which the whole operation was dubbed, went like this: around 7 A.M. a briefing would be held of all the squads to share information/intelligence. The hours following this briefing were spent by each squad running down leads arising from the day's itinerary, and at night another briefing was held sharing information/intelligence gathered during that particular day – as well as a formal update of what was being uncovered in Oklahoma.

The overall overseer of the OKBOMB task force was Special Agent in Charge David Tubbs (SA*IC* – the FBI didn't use the familiar term "SAC" because of its sexual connotation). SAIC Tubbs proved a very capable leader, and would go on to brighter days within the FBI because of the success he had at OKBOMB.

The Shit Squad found us (the Denver ATF agents) teamed up with some very capable and seasoned FBI agents from all over the country. They were primarily members of the FBI Surveillance Operations Division (SOD). This unit was a crack squad that specialized in the surreptitious installation of wiretaps and counter surveillance maneuvers.

For example, if SOD was assigned the job of installing wiretaps or secret recording devices in a structure, some agents would do the actual wiring while others sat on the street in cars to be used as "blockers" should any bad guys venture home early. They would then stage mock traffic accidents or other such diversions to preclude anyone from dropping in and discovering the electronic installation(s). In all, these guys were experts, and I don't use that term lightly. Over the coming weeks I became amazed at the proficiency of this unit.

Each ATF agent was teamed up with one SOD agent, and we would in turn follow leads and try to learn where the ammonium nitrate had been procured. I was teamed with an FBI agent named Dave, and we would become good friends and great partners. Dave was also a maniac when it came to driving, obviously learned during the many years of being in SOD. Riding in a car with Dave was like riding with Jeff Gordon at Talladega. I don't think Dave ever drove under 100mph, and this was a good thing, for there were days where we'd have to cover 500 miles or more. So, getting from one town to another took little or no time, though we were pulled over by the Kansas State Patrol almost daily. These officers became friends of ours and soon gave us *carte blanche* in driving the many roads of rural Kansas. I almost wished they hadn't, for I was sure I would soon die with Dave behind the wheel. Miraculously, that never happened – he was always in control.

At first we were instructed by SAIC Tubbs to only search back a few months (roughly to January 1995) to see if anyone had ever purchased a large amount of NH_4NO_3 during that time frame. As I would soon learn from dealers in fertilizer, such a large purchase was extremely rare, for most farmers didn't use such large amounts of ammonium nitrate as fertilizer, due to storage and theft issues. NH_4NO_3 , though very stable (it could only be used as an explosive when "boosted" by other explosives – procurement of which was assigned to another squad), it wasn't usually the first fertilizer choice of farmers; most used urea, another nitrogen variant, $(NH_2)_2CO$, that was more conducive to huge fertilization jobs. This fact made our search a little easier, though it would take some time for us to finally find the dealer who had made the actual sale(s) to the suspects.

After some time it became apparent that the perpetrators had not purchased the NH_4NO_3 during the time frame we investigated – at least not in the state of Kansas. This was discouraging. However, a subsequent search warrant of Terry Nichols' residence yielded a sales receipt for the purchase of a full palette of ammonium nitrate that had been made in the fall of 1994. There were countless search warrants applied for and executed at Nichols' home, but it took one of the later searches to uncover the sales slip.

We were then instructed to focus our search all the way back to the summer of 1994 and work our way forward from that point. It was then that we were able to find the second purchase, also made during the fall of 1994. The Shit Squad had come through with glowing colors. We had done our job and would subsequently do any duty given to us. Everyone at the OKBOMB task force was appreciative of our work. Each mini-unit of the Shit Squad covered thousands of miles canvassing Kansas for the source of the fertilizer, and if it wasn't for the open sharing of information between all squads, our scope would have remained very limited.

As stated, everyone was appreciative of our work, but no one more than FBI Director Louis Freeh who personally came to Ft. Riley to show his personal appreciation to each and every agent and staff worker – FBI or otherwise. Director Freeh met with every person assigned to OKBOMB, and his mere presence made us all feel extremely proud.

I mention this fact because during our entire five-week assignment at Ft. Riley, not one ATF higher-up ever made the trip to Junction City to express his appreciation. None of us were looking for a pat on the back, but being so far removed from home and away from our loved ones did take a toll. Besides, our immediate bosses were in Kansas City which was only two hours away! We never saw any of them; in fact, an interim ASAC (Assistant Special Agent in Charge) had been designated on site to be our immediate boss at OKBOMB – thus precluding the SAC or any other ATF bigwig from having to make the journey.

None of the ATF agents could understand this, but it didn't really matter because we were now working for the United States, not any one agency. Still, I learned a lot about ATF during those days. I had a great conversation with Director Freeh that day and will always cherish the moment. He honestly knew the historical significance of the case and cared. My superiors? Who knows.

While at Ft. Riley, an explosive incident arose in the town of Concordia, which is northwest of Junction City and about eighty miles by car. Apparently, some guy had a house full of explosives, and Ben and I were instructed to go up there to investigate. There was one problem however: this was during a torrential rainstorm. If you've never seen or been in a Midwest rainstorm, then you haven't seen anything. That eighty miles became the eighty miles from hell – shit, I felt like I was sailing around Cape Horn! I don't know how long it took to get to Concordia but I'm thankful Ben was driving.

When we arrived we were met by some local cops who said they had arrested a guy earlier that day that had broken some law – I can't remember. When the officers subsequently went into the guy's house they saw in plain view all kinds of shit, including what could have been massive pipe bombs.

I asked if a bomb squad or EOD (Explosives Ordnance Disposal) had been contacted at Ft. Riley, and I was told they were on the way. When the bomb squad finally arrived I learned something that hadn't been told to me by the initial responders: the local officers had not cleared the entire house. After entering and seeing potential bombs and contraband, they made haste and got out of the residence. In other words, it was still possible that someone could have been inside.

Moreover, Ben and I were told by the bomb squad that it would not go into the house until it was "Code 4," or clear. What that translated into was Ben and I would have to clear the whole house. Now, I was not a bomb freak and neither was Ben, but we had no alternative. Though the chances were slim, we would have to look in every nook and cranny of the residence to see if anyone was in there.

The rain had finally stopped (thank God), but I was scared shitless! Apparently the suspect was a survivalist-type who was anti-government and anti-just-about-everything. Kind of like McVeigh and Nichols.

So, Ben and I began clearing the house. Carefully. In the living room were anti-government publications, military ordnance manuals, and all kinds of explosives periodicals. After clearing the upstairs, Ben and I descended into the basement. I remember the stairway was tight and unstable, and as we made our descent we began to see all kinds of shit. The basement contained black powder canisters, military ammunition containers, huge PVC pipe concoctions – everything you'd expect in a bomb-making factory. By this time I was pissing in my pants out of fear – knowing that just touching the wrong item could blow the entire house off the map. Ben and I cleared the room (for people, that is) and slowly made our way back up the stairs and to the street.

Outside we met with the bomb squad and told them what we had seen. At that time the locals took no chances; they evacuated the entire block should anything go wrong. The bomb squad subsequently sent a robot in to go through all the suspected PVC pipe bombs in the basement, but the search proved negative. The suspect had everything to make explosives devices, but he hadn't assembled any.

Storage issues were another story. You can't just keep this stuff in a closet in your basement, so I think the guy eventually got prosecuted for storage violations as well as having a combination of parts to make a bomb. A local ATF agent eventually took over the investigation, but Ben and I had done all the legwork – and thank God I still *had* my legs after walking through that explosives den. That was one of the scariest episodes I'd ever been involved in, but hey, that's why I got paid.

As the weeks grew into a month at Ft. Riley, we all realized the historic importance of our work and the work of everyone at OKBOMB as well as at Oklahoma City. When we arrived at Ft. Riley, the case against Nichols was weak at best, despite the obvious and not-so-apparent connections made to McVeigh. After leaving Junction City five weeks later, the case against Nichols was a done deal; he would be toast when it came to the ensuing prosecution.

We would all soon return home and prepare for the trials, ironically to occur in Denver after the venue of the case was subsequently moved there. I won't get into the court proceedings, because the facts and circumstances have been well-documented. However, being that the Denver Federal Building was an almost exact facsimile of the Murrah building, one can only imagine the security applied to the Denver edifice. The trials took place in 1997, and Timothy McVeigh was subsequently sentenced to death, and Terry Nichols was given life without parole. Several other accomplices were also convicted and sent to federal prison.

Though the initial tragedy was beyond egregious, the aftermath and working relationships forged were a grand example of how justice could be served and all attitudes and preconceived notions put aside for the better of a common goal.

And, for those who feel that McVeigh and Nichols were treated like Nazi POW's while in federal custody, one tidbit needs to be stated. McVeigh and Nichols were given their own "apartments" in the basement of the Denver Federal Building – lodgings that were better than any apartment I had ever lived in, minus the lockdown aspect. Both were allowed to order any type of food during the trials, and both were treated with the utmost respect and decorum. They didn't deserve it, but they got it anyway.

Appreciation here needs to be given to the United States Marshal's Service, specifically Group Supervisor Bobby Lloyd – a good friend of mine, who arranged and supervised the temporary lodgings. The fantastic job the USMS performed would take an entire book to relate; just know that like all the other agencies involved in the whole affair, it performed magnificently.

OKBOMB remains one of the most significant investigations I had the pleasure of working, but it wouldn't be my greatest accomplishment as a federal agent. That would arise soon after returning to Denver, as I became privy to a lone woman who was buying a multitude of firearms. These guns would soon be turning up all over the streets of metropolitan Denver as well as out-of-state, notably metropolitan Los Angeles.

The ensuing case, again with LA ties, would soon propel me into the den of murderous gangbangers, soulless criminals who would stop at nothing to kill, including law enforcement officers.

Chapter XVI

Drive-thru Gun Shop

When it comes to entrepreneurship, the following individual has to be at or near the top of the list. Donald Trump would have been proud. After the Brady Law was enacted in 1994, the new *modus operandi* among new "businessmen" who had no criminal record was to buy large quantities of firearms (mostly lower-end handguns) and branch out as new undocumented dealers. The Brady legislation also upped the dealer licensing fee from $30 for three years to $200. Not a huge jump by market standards, but what rising young commercial star wants to deal with the paperwork?! Enter Raja*.

After Brady and while stationed in Denver, I partnered with the Aurora Police Department's (APD) Pawn Unit who amassed pawn and sales slips from local pawn shops on their firearm sales. Colorado had no state gun registry at the time (unlike California and many other states), but a local ordinance required all pawn establishments to report their gun sales and pawns to APD. These slips were picked up weekly by APD.

Per capita, Aurora, Colorado, has to rank among the top five U.S. cities having pawn shops, and for some reason most criminals do business with such infamous storefronts. Like most pawnshops, there are good and bad ones, and by bad I mean they'd sell firearms to anyone, despite any tell-tale signs that the purchaser may be a little sketchy. As long as the latter individual passed the criminal background check as mandated by Brady, the person could buy as many guns he or she wanted. Unbeknownst to the buyers in Aurora, APD monitored these sales.

As did I. Enter again, Raja.

Thanks to APD's Pawn Unit, I got onto him after he had purchased more than 50 handguns and a few rifles. The handguns were all low-end pistols: Brycos, Lorcins, Davises, etc. This is another tell-tale sign of people dealing without a federal firearms license. Most Big-5's and legitimate gun dealers – over 90 per cent are legit – don't make much money from selling such "garbage." However, on the street these types of firearms were like gold.

One could buy a Lorcin .25 caliber pistol for $50 and turn around and sell it on the street for as much as $200. Ah, the wafting of capitalism. Raja took advantage of this. What he couldn't gauge was how many of these guns would turn up in crime scenes all over the metropolitan Denver area.

I tracked every serial number for weeks, and as sure as the sun sets in the west, multiple weapons began to turn up in many crimes. This gave me leverage when I approached the "dealer" who held no FFL.

It took some time to locate Raja (he had listed a bogus address when purchasing), and in looking for him I wasn't sure what I would find. He had a unique Middle-Eastern or Central Asian name and surname, so I wasn't really sure if I was chasing an ordinary street hustler or an expatriate Sikh militant. Turned out it was the former. It was through employment records that I was finally able to track him down.

I have to admit, he remains one of the few criminals I've ever hunted or worked that actually held a legitimate job, that is, if you consider flipping burgers at the local Burger World* an aspiring profession. As it turned out, my partners and I were able to set up surveillance on numerous occasions at Raja's workplace.

One late night (he only worked such ungodly hours) I ventured in for a burger and fries and came face to face with this young entrepreneur. He was a young Black male – 21 or 22 – skinny, whose hair was receding like someone much older. He seemed harmless enough, but most of them do, and on this particular night we were able to follow him to his residence. Previous efforts had proved negative.

The next day an Aurora Gang Officer and I visited Raja at his humble apartment. By humble, I remember there only being a torn-up couch in the messy studio. We identified ourselves and I began to question Raja on his recent and numerous gun purchases. Raja was very open, even polite, and said that he indeed was selling the guns to make some extra cash. Considering that he'd spent over $2000 in cash in furthering this venture, I asked where the money came from. He honestly said that many times friends would loan him the cash and he would make the purchases.

After reciting the federal licensing requirement for such commerce, I told him that his gun-dealing days were now over, and if he continued I would throw him in federal prison for dealing without a license, a ten-year beef, as well as make him an accessory for the many crimes his guns had subsequently been involved in.

He got the idea, for he never bought another gun I knew of. Then again, he didn't have much of an opportunity, since he was murdered soon afterward in an unsolved gangland slaying. Another example of lying down with dogs and waking up with fleas. However, there is an interesting twist to the story.

It was sometime later, after Raja's death, that I ran into several cohorts of his during the course of my duties. It was then that I learned that not only did Raja buy guns for specific people, but at times he also sold firearms out of the drive-thru window at Burger World! My respect for him, albeit posthumous, rose tremendously.

I could just see it: a carload of gangbangers ordering combo meals at the drive-thru and receiving the ultimate toy for their happy meal purchases. "Yeah, I'll have a cheeseburger, large fries, a coke, and how 'bout a Lorcin .380." What a novel idea!

The added temerity of this escapade didn't escape my partners or boss, who definitely let it be known to me that many of these "sales" had happened right under my very nose as I looked on. No wonder some of those paper bags looked so heavy. Anyway, Raja cast a shadow, but now rests easily in a local graveyard. R.I.P. young entrepreneur; you'll never be forgotten.

Chapter XVII

First Blood

I need to preface this chapter by saying its content details my most important and proudest achievement as an ATF agent, though it has nothing to do with an arrest, a long sentencing, or the recovery of boatloads of evidence. It deals with something more important, human life. I never received any commendations from ATF over the case's ultimate outcome, which is still ongoing, but I didn't seek any.

I never had the pleasure of working for a local police department, whose universal objective is "to protect and serve"; yet, this creed imbedded itself in the back of my brain from day one. The preceding chapters may not indicate that, but rest assured, it was omnipresent.

It was around winter 1997 that I returned to my old duties of tracking illegal firearms purchasers. This put me on the trail of a female who had purchased in excess of sixty handguns, a telltale indicator. All were low-end pistols, the primary choice of the gangbanger, and each purchase had taken place at a suspect pawn shop in Aurora.

At first I didn't have a lot of leverage on the woman, so I waited for some of the guns to turn up in crime scenes, which, like clockwork, they soon did. Many of the firearms found their way into police reports which documented just about every crime you could envision; some even turned up on the streets of metropolitan Los Angeles. Again I had my LA nexus and I dove into the ensuing investigation. The woman's name was Regina Marks*, and although I didn't know it at the time, she would figure in my life forever.

The pawn shop in question was named Georgia Pawn*, probably because the men who ran the business were from one of the former Soviet Socialist Republics. I had dealt with the owners on numerous occasions and got to know them quite well. They were always cordial with me, but I was playing them.

Another agent in my office had initiated a full federal firearms licensee (FFL) investigation into Georgia Pawn. The business was suspected of performing illegal sales and selling to many "undesirables." An inordinate number of Georgia Pawn guns were turning up in police reports all over the country which was a good indicator that something fishy was going on.

FFL investigations were very sensitive within ATF, due to Second Amendment issues and the power of the National Rifle Association lobby, and ATF Headquarters monitored these cases closely. Therefore, any time I went into the business to retrieve records or just shoot the breeze, I was always full of smiles and cordialities. I didn't want to give any indication that ATF was working a case on the business.

Ben Maxwell and I had originally initiated the investigation into Georgia Pawn, but the case was soon handed off to another agent in our office who was seeking a promotion. This case and its finality were sure to get him that pay raise, so we had no problem giving it to his direction.

The problem was, the case agent Russell Brandt* didn't work the case with the same assiduity and thoroughness that Ben and I had. Brandt was on the ATF SWAT team and was on travel status sometimes three weeks out of every month; as a result, the Georgia Pawn case dragged on for years.

During this time I began working "straw buyers" who made purchases from the pawn shop. A "straw buyer" was a person who actually filled out the paperwork at the gun store, passed the criminal background check, and then gave or sold the guns to a second person. Most gun shops were on the watch for straw purchasers, and would usually turn them away if any particular transaction seemed suspect. Georgia Pawn, on the other hand, didn't give two shits who the *actual* buyer was; as long as the paperwork and background check were kosher, then the store knew it would be extremely hard for the Feds to make any case against them challenging the sales(s).

Georgia Pawn was also very overt about its practices: there were times when five or six gangbangers would walk into the store, pick out the guns *they* wanted, have their girlfriend fill out all the paperwork and pass the background check, hand her the money, have her give the cash to the clerk, and then the whole brood would exit the store with the firearms. It didn't take a brain surgeon to figure out that these types of transactions were suspect at best, but as long as no one took notice, the sales were consummated.

For Brandt to actually develop a good case against Georgia Pawn, he would have to do numerous controlled purchases (i.e., utilizing audio and video monitoring) where these types of sham sales were documented. He specifically chose an out-of-state undercover agent to accompany any confidential informant – usually a woman – into the store to perform the straw purchases. Since the undercover agent made it known to the owners that he was from out-of-state, the sales were illegal, *per se*, because a non-resident of a state could not buy a handgun. Brandt's plan was to make numerous purchases with the undercover agent, record the buys to show that Georgia Pawn was in habit of conducting these types of sales, and eventually take them down. But as stated, Brandt was gone most of the time, and adding to the fact that the undercover agent was from out of state, his FFL investigation proceeded at a snail's pace.

I, on the other hand, began targeting other straw purchasers who were buying from Georgia Pawn. I had an accordion folder in my office with dozens of individuals I suspected were making straw purchases. This information was mostly gleaned from the Aurora PD Pawn Unit and its records. I subsequently wrote many federal firearms cases against the straw buyers as well as the criminals these people were buying for, but I had to throw all the case reports (the final packet we would submit to the United States Attorney's Office) in a drawer. I couldn't go forward with my cases because it jeopardized Brandt's FFL case.

I knew that if I pursued any of these cases before Brandt's case was finalized, I'd be putting myself between a rock and a hard place. I knew the first question I would get from any defense attorney or grand jury member would be: "Well, aren't you (ATF) working the dealer in this case?" What was I going to say?

I couldn't lie to a grand jury (though I had no problem bending the truth when it came to defense attorneys), but that didn't matter. I knew any defense attorney would send its own investigators out to interview the employees of Georgia Pawn. This would probably be enough for the pawn shop to cool its illicit practices, at least for some time. So, I could do nothing until Brandt completed his overall "umbrella" case.

As a result I left many criminals and firearms on the street to continually turn up in crime scenes all over the country. This played on my conscience hard, and I urged my boss at the time to light a fire under Brandt's ass because sooner or later, one of the shitheads I left on the street was going to kill someone. That statement would play itself out later in huge fashion.

As stated, a woman by the name of Regina Marks was making numerous handgun purchases from Georgia Pawn, and at the very least she needed to be approached and told to stop. As to who she was buying for, I could develop another case report to subsequently throw in my desk drawer awaiting Brandt's case completion. Little did I know, this case would have legs of its own, of which I would have a hell of a time keeping pace.

One afternoon in the fall of 1997, my partner Don Goren* and I decided to approach Ms. Marks. Through pawn records we knew she lived in a rundown apartment in Aurora, and though we had attempted to contact her in the past, we had always missed her. This day she was finally home. I knocked at the door and a buxom white woman answered. We identified ourselves and asked her if it would be alright if we spoke to her about her recent gun purchases. She cordially assented and let us into her apartment.

There wasn't much furniture in the place, and the residence was fairly unkempt. I also noticed that a young boy was playing with some toys on the living room floor; he couldn't have been more than four or five. Ms. Marks told us that the boy was her son Lucas, and that he was five years-old. Don and I sat down at a dinette table with Marks and began our questioning.

She was very nice and told us everything. She stated that she had been purchasing all the handguns for a Crip gang member named Rambo, and that she had been forced to perform all the buys under extreme duress. Translation: if she had refused she would have been killed by Rambo. She was also forced to do other things not worth relating. Moreover, her son Lucas was usually with her when all this activity took place.

It was a moving story. She also had the receipts from every purchase she had made. When asked what each buy usually entailed, she detailed how Rambo and his crew would just show up at her apartment, throw her and Lucas in a van or other vehicle, and travel down to Georgia Pawn. When asked why they always went to Georgia Pawn, she stated because Rambo supposedly knew the owners. I knew this intelligence would figure prominently in Brandt's FFL case when the time came for him to use it.

When asked if she knew Rambo's real name, she said she did not. That didn't matter, because I knew it wouldn't be difficult finding out who this guy was. She said he was originally from California – Compton she thought – but had relocated to the Denver metropolitan area. He was in his early 20's, if that, and scared the living hell out of her.

When asked about each individual purchase, Marks recalled every minute detail; her memory was uncanny. She, Rambo, and the crew would go into Georgia Pawn, where the gangbangers would select all the guns while Marks filled out the paperwork and passed the background check. They would even pay the clerks directly and carry the guns out of the store by themselves! Lucas was usually left in the car or at the apartment under the "care" of another gangbanger.

Again, I knew this information would make Brandt ecstatic though it made me extremely sick to my stomach. Marks said that after completing all the purchases, the crew would then drive to a storage locker somewhere in Aurora, and all the guns would be deposited there. The gangsters would then drive her and Lucas back to their apartment and dump them off.

I asked her if she ever received any payment for the purchases, and she replied sometimes she would be flipped a little cash or something else – though usually nothing was exchanged – only the intangible guarantee that she would remain alive. My hatred for Rambo and these clowns grew exponentially each minute she related her story.

Time soon came for Don and I to leave, but I told Marks I would be in touch. I also told her to try to stay away from Rambo if at all possible. Since she didn't work, she said she could often stay with some relatives and keep away from her apartment. I told her I thought that was a good idea. We soon left with knots in our guts over what had just been related to us.

But I knew I was on to something good.

In the ensuing weeks I began researching Rambo but only hit dead ends. There was no record of that moniker in Denver or Aurora, probably because he was from Compton and had stayed under the radar in Colorado. I had fellow agents try to run down the moniker in Los Angeles, but there were hundreds of Rambo's. Go figure. I guess they were big Stallone fans.

I spoke with Regina Marks often, especially about the location of the storage locker in Aurora. She couldn't pinpoint the locale but would try to remember. I asked her if she'd been contacted by Rambo since my visit, but she said she had not, though she had received telephone calls from him which she didn't return. I instructed her to continue this practice.

The big break in identifying Rambo came one afternoon when I received a call from Marks. She told me that Rambo had come over to her apartment but surprisingly not to have her buy guns. Rather, he had her accompany him to a local grocery store to make a wire transfer of cash to California. During this transaction the true name of Rambo came to light: his name was Randy Canister. Marks had a keen photographic memory, and she relayed this intelligence to me that afternoon. I would soon begin filling my dossier on every bit of information I could get on Canister, and the file began to fill up quite quickly. Canister was, I think, 20 years of age – which precluded him from purchasing handguns (one had to be 21); yet, his adult criminal history was sparse – unusual for anyone from Los Angeles, especially Compton.

As I dug deeper, I did learn that his juvenile record was quite extensive, though I would not be able to use any of this information in federal court during any subsequent court proceedings. So, I didn't have a lot of history (or leverage) on Rambo, but I knew there had to be something all the paper records weren't telling me.

Soon thereafter I contacted an Aurora PD detective friend who was the "Wikipedia" of gang information. His name was Stephon Blanton*, and he knew everything about every gangbanger in the metropolitan Denver area and even Los Angeles. Through Blanton I would learn all about Rambo's gang (the Corner Pocket Crips), his associates, his girlfriends (who were also gang members), everything. He provided me with contacts, addresses, all sorts of information. I would soon learn that despite the fact that Canister had kept his record fairly clean in Colorado, he was nevertheless a pretty bad dude. That made me want to take him down even more.

It was several weeks later, in the latter part of November 1997, that I learned Regina Marks had made another purchase of firearms from Georgia Pawn; this information was passed on to me, not by her, but by the Aurora PD Pawn Unit. The buy had occurred about a week before I received the intelligence. I tried to contact Marks but had no luck.

I quickly flagged all the newly-purchased serial numbers in the ATF Suspect Gun Database (SGD); I had done this for all the guns previously purchased as well. Through the SGD, anytime one of the flagged serial numbers turned up in a police report anywhere in the country, I would be notified. I would subsequently notify the reporting police department and procure a police report of what had occurred and how the firearm(s) had been recovered.

It wasn't a day after that I was quickly notified by ATF Headquarters that three guns from the latest Marks purchase had turned up in south central Los Angeles, and they had been recovered only five days after the buy! Moreover, they had been recovered from three fellow gangbangers in Rambo's gang. Obviously, Canister had trafficked the firearms to California, a major felony offense. I now had him if only I could map out the time frame and nexus from purchase to the recovery in LA. I knew a lot of work still needed to be done, but this revelation was huge.

I knew I had to find Marks.

My partner Don and I finally located her at home soon afterward. I asked her why she hadn't contacted me about the recent purchase, but she said she had been scared for her life. I cut her some slack, for I had begun to feel the shadow cast by Canister. Marks did have some good information however; she told me where the storage locker was because they had all gone there to deposit the guns after the buy and she paid special notice this time. Don and I subsequently went to the storage facility and were able to confirm that Randy Canister did in fact rent a storage unit under his own name at the complex. I now knew that I needed to act.

I soon approached my boss and filled him in on all the recent developments in the Rambo case. I told him that I thought I could get a federal search warrant for the storage unit, do the warrant execution for only intelligence purposes, and not endanger Brandt's overall Georgia Pawn case. I told my supervisor that if we did find firearms in the unit, we could take them without leaving any trail leading back to Marks. The guns would be off the street, and the only issue Canister would have would be with the storage facility or with his accomplices.

I was presumably putting the owners of the storage complex in jeopardy, but I took that chance. If anything they could make the whole thing look like a burglary of the unit should we recover a lot of evidence; that was a common occurrence at such places. My boss agreed, and Brandt had no problem with the plan. I subsequently wrote and obtained a federal search warrant for the storage shed.

The next day we decided to execute the warrant.

There was snow on the ground that afternoon, and it was briskly cold. When we arrived at the complex we were let in by the clerk and proceeded to Canister's unit. After popping the lock we ventured inside. It was a large unit, perhaps 10' x 20', and big enough to hold a car, as evidenced by a broken-down vehicle inside the unit. The place was littered with all kinds of material, including gang photos, miscellaneous papers, and many gun boxes. We took down the information off the boxes but left them in the unit. We also found two firearms: one from a previous purchase and one for which I had no record. In all, we left the place pretty much the way we had found it.

I was somewhat disappointed on what we did (or didn't) find, for I was hoping there'd be a lot of firearms in the place. By federal law I was required to leave an inventory of everything we had taken, which I did, but I was easily able to stash the inventory under some papers and crap strewn about the storage unit. We soon wrapped up our enforcement operation and began driving back to the office.

Driving back downtown I quickly received a call from Don. Don said that as soon as he had left the complex he had received a call from the facility's owner and operator. He told Don that Canister was currently at the storage complex inquiring about why the lock had been removed from his unit.

Don and another agent quickly returned to the complex and confronted Canister. The cat was now out of the bag. Somewhat. Canister was detained by these agents until I could get back to the scene. My mind was now racing a mile a minute, and I knew I had to do something with Canister. All sorts of scenarios began racing through my head, and I made the decision to arrest him. I didn't care what Brandt or my supervisor would say; I just knew this fuckhead needed to be off the street.

As I got back to the storage facility I had my first encounter with Rambo. It wouldn't be my last and definitely not the most memorable, but I had to come up with a story and fast. I don't remember what charge I arrested him on that afternoon, but I believe it had to do with his underage status and his involvement in one or more of the Marks purchases of handguns. We hooked him on the spot and transported him downtown to our office for processing.

As soon as the "bracelets" were affixed to Rambo's wrists, I knew I had to do something with Regina Marks and her son. And quickly! Otherwise, they would be dead. I quickly got hold of her and had several agents go to her apartment and move her and her son for the time being to a motel on the other side of town. This would buy me some time, though not a lot, for the cards were on the table.

Canister would soon be able to put two and two together and figure out that Marks was the reason for his arrest. I also knew that Rambo would at a minimum be in federal custody for three days pending a detention/bond hearing. This bought me three additional days. I would have to write a Criminal Complaint charging him with federal firearms violations, and after presenting that document to a federal Magistrate Judge, I would then have to get all my ducks in a row.

In the meantime, that which was paramount was the safety of Marks and her young son. The rest was only paperwork.

When we got downtown we took Canister up to our office on the sixth floor and began our prisoner processing. This entailed procuring fingerprints from the suspect as well as filling out a personal information sheet. At that time the suspect is *Mirandized* (if not done earlier) and asked if he/she would like to talk to the arresting agents without an attorney. Canister stated that he wished to have a lawyer present, and no questioning took place – only fingerprinting and the completion of the personal information document.

It was after this processing that I would truly learn who Randy Canister was. His visage was horrifying and caused me to flash back to my high school years when I had been mugged by a couple of Crips in Los Angeles. As stated in the Prologue, I learned a valuable street lesson that night. Even with a gun to my head I knew I was safe – that those two thugs weren't going to kill me. But as I looked Canister in the eye that afternoon, I saw exactly the opposite.

I knew that if he ever had the chance to pull the trigger, then he would do so – and with no remorse. Ask any true agent who has worked the streets and he'll tell you: you get to learn, after dealing with so many shitheads, who the real badasses are. I knew by looking into Rambo's eyes that he was one. It frightened the hell out of me, but I knew everyone concerned was at least safe for the moment. Canister was in federal custody and would be so for three days – and hopefully longer. But I knew a time would soon come to act, and act fast, should he receive bond.

That night I completed a Criminal Complaint and forwarded it to the United States Attorney's Office, and the case was assigned to an Assistant United States Attorney (AUSA). Canister was taken before a federal Magistrate Judge the next morning and subsequently remanded to the custody of the US Marshal's Service pending the detention hearing to be held in three days. During the entire Initial Appearance I saw the same stoic and passionless gaze emanating from Rambo's eyes. He only smirked, answered a few questions put to him by the court, and lifelessly gazed about the courtroom.

I had never witnessed such deportment from anyone in my career – criminal or otherwise – and as I said earlier, it terrified me. I knew this guy needed to stay behind bars, and not just for the sake of Regina

Marks and her son, but for society in general. It's hard to explain to someone who hasn't witnessed it. He had an almost John Gotti-like demeanor about him, but without all the pomp and drama. He was as calm as a mountain tarn at daybreak. I would never forget it.

The day of Canister's Initial Appearance I was called into a meeting with my boss, Brandt, and every agent who had participated in Rambo's arrest. We also had several AUSAs listening in on a conference call. A strategy needed to be formulated on how to handle the Canister case without jeopardizing the Georgia Pawn investigation, which was still light years from finalization. It was agreed that Canister would be charged, but should the case ever jeopardize the Georgia Pawn investigation, then another strategy would have to be formulated. All parties agreed, and I began preparing for Rambo's detention hearing. Hopefully the Magistrate Judge would deny him bail, thus keeping him locked up pending all subsequent hearings and proceedings, including trial. That usually was a coin flip.

For the next few days I had Regina Marks watched around the clock. We bought her and Lucas food, and tried to make their lives as normal as possible (which in hindsight seems laughable). I assured her that nothing would happen to her and that she would be formally relocated pending all court proceedings. Odds were always good that a case like this would not go to trial because the defendant would plead guilty to charges precluding trial. I knew the case against Canister was weak at best; if convicted he would probably only receive a year or eighteen months in federal prison. Yet, that was better than nothing. I knew we could possibly go after him at a later date when the whole Georgia Pawn case was presented. At the time it was the best we could do.

The morning after the meeting in my office I had all of Marks's belongings moved out of her apartment to temporary storage. Like the Grinch, we left nothing. We didn't even notify the landlord; we just got everything out.

That afternoon Don and I had a late lunch out by the apartment and decided to drive by the residence. Don was driving, and so as not to bring any attention, we drove up the alley behind the complex. As we neared the apartment, Don and I saw four large black males exiting a tan Ford Taurus behind the residence. They looked sketchy to say the least, so Don decided to drive completely through the alley and circle back whereupon we would confront these suspects. I don't even think I had my gun, but I didn't care; these guys needed to be shaken down.

As we made our way back into the alley we soon noticed that the Ford Taurus was gone. There was no one to be found. We drove around the area for a good time looking for the vehicle, but luck was apparently on the side of the criminals. What did become apparent to both of us was that those guys hadn't been at the Marks apartment to deliver the mail. They had definitely been there with other intentions.

Again, I was witness to the shadow cast by Randy Canister and the Corner Pocket Crips.

The next day, the day before the detention hearing, I was called into my boss' office. He shut the door, which was never a good sign. I asked what was up and was soon told by my supervisor that Rambo was going to be released by the US Attorney's Office; the jeopardy to the Georgia Pawn case was too great. Besides, we could come back later and still prosecute Canister. I was flabbergasted! I had already left several criminals on the street because of Georgia Pawn, but enough was enough. I told my boss that I understood the reasoning, but if anyone needed to be in jail, it was Canister. He had already tried to kill Marks, and I knew he would stop at nothing in trying to locate her, which in all reality was a pipe dream but a threat nonetheless. I pleaded with my boss, but he would hear nothing of it. The criminal complaint was to be dropped and Rambo was to be released before any detention hearing took place. Hours later he was released with all charges dropped. I was stunned.

I was now only left with Regina Marks and her son. Breaking the news to them of Rambo's release from federal custody was painful to say the least, but I assured her that she would be moved to a safe area, probably out of town. She trusted my judgment, which was good, but having to deal with her and Lucas became a real pain in the ass at times.

Over the ensuing months I bounced her around from place to place, from city to city, until I was finally able to find a small apartment which I knew would be safe. All of this cost ATF a sizable amount of money, but I didn't give a shit. I spent the money regardless, and ironically would have to explain my actions to the brass at a later date because I apparently used monies out of the wrong fund. I had to write a formal memorandum detailing why I had done what I had done, and that became the end of it, though not without verbal chastisement from the higher-ups. Such is ATF administrative policy.

By now we were well into 1998, but no one could have foreseen what would transpire later that year. Six months or so after Canister was released on my case, three individuals were executed in a drug deal gone bad in south Aurora. Another person had been shot but had miraculously survived. The victims were tied up, some sexually assaulted, and executed in brutal gangland fashion.

Three Crip gangbangers would eventually be apprehended and charged with the murders, Randy Canister among them. Another of the suspected killers, Dante Jones, had been one of the gangsters arrested with one of the Regina Marks guns in November 1997. The nexus was now totally out in the open. Canister, Jones, and another accomplice, Trevon Washington, would be tried and sentenced in Arapahoe County Superior Court. Canister received the death penalty, but this would later be commuted to life in prison without parole.

The irony here (or tragedy, depending on how you looked at it) was had Rambo been held and tried in my case, odds were good these murders never would have taken place – at least not by Canister because he would have been in federal prison. I brought this up to my superiors and the United States Attorney's Office, but no one seemed to care.

Again, I was flabbergasted, though not surprised. Though I didn't think Rambo would take it to that level, I knew he was dangerous; his eyes told the true tale. I had urged my bosses to keep him locked up and to prosecute him, but to them the Georgia Pawn case was always more important.

More irony (or tragedy): the Georgia Pawn case did finally go to prosecution in federal court in 2000, but the case was subsequently dropped; Georgia Pawn only had to surrender its firearms license, though it was allowed to sell all remaining guns in its inventory, which was plentiful. Such is justice at the federal level. I thought state court was a joke, but at least it would hand out felony convictions with little or no prison time. The federal attorneys wouldn't even pursue that.

Again, it was all a big lie.

As stated at the beginning of this chapter, this episode highlights my greatest achievement as an ATF federal agent, and not because of anything to do with Rambo. It has to do with Regina Marks and her son Lucas. Over the ensuing years I would receive countless thank you notes, pictures, Christmas cards, and sometimes birthday cards from her and her son. I got to witness Regina get her life together and for Lucas to grow up into a young man.

Even this past year, 2010, I was happy to receive a high school graduation announcement from Lucas. He was graduating and was looking ahead to college. Nothing has ever made me more proud, for I know I had a hand in that kid having a chance in life. My love for his mother and him is immeasurable and never-ending, and we remain in contact to this very day despite the fact that I no longer work for ATF.

These pages are for you two more than anyone.

Chapter XVIII

Judge For Yourself

Here's yet another illustration of how stupid criminals can be. One day Ben Maxwell and I were sitting in the office and a call came in from a citizen who claimed one of his co-workers wanted to sell some machineguns. Most "cold" calls we received were bogus, so we didn't lend much weight to this guy's story, but Ben and I decided to follow up on it. We subsequently met the individual at a local restaurant, and he told us that a co-worker of his, an ex-Army GI, could modify semi-automatic firearms into fully-automatic weapons. He provided us with the suspect's name, and Ben and I subsequently did as much background investigation into this guy as we could. After doing so, it became apparent that the concerned citizen was providing corroborative information.

Soon thereafter, Ben instructed the citizen to arrange a meeting between the suspect, Dick Welles*, and two undercover ATF agents – Ben and me. The meet was coordinated to take place in a local park, and several days later the rendezvous occurred. Ben and I were on the ultimate alert, for we weren't sure what to expect. The initial meeting between undercovers and criminals is always tenuous at best, so we had our game faces on.

The encounter was scheduled for 2 P.M., and prior to our arrival, numerous cover agents situated themselves in and around the area. I wore an electronic transmitter to monitor all conversation. We also brought a sizable amount of cash, just to show Welles that we were serious buyers. We didn't expect him to bring any hardware – no criminal would do that on an initial meet – but we just wanted to let Welles know our word was good.

We arrived punctually at the park at 2 P.M. and found Welles and the citizen already there, standing next to a full-sized pickup. Welles was a thin white male, probably thirty years old, and his mannerisms fit the description of a military man. After some small talk the conversation turned to the subject of machineguns.

After talking for maybe fifteen minutes, it became apparent that Welles knew what he was talking about in reference to machinegun conversions. We negotiated a price, thinking that the actual deal would be made on a later date. To our surprise Welles pulled a MAC-10 pistol out of his truck and showed it to us. He stated that he had converted the gun from semi-automatic fire (i.e., one round expended with each trigger pull) to fully-automatic, or one trigger pull to expend the entire magazine of ammunition. He even let Ben hold it and field-test it to see if it was indeed fully-automatic. This act can be done in lieu of any ammunition or firing range, and after Ben was done screwing around with the weapon, he confirmed that it was indeed fully-automatic.

Though our faces didn't show it, we were flabbergasted that any criminal would display his wares to total strangers on an initial meet, but it soon became obvious that this guy needed the cash. Some more small talk ensued, and the buy was made. Welles and the citizen left with the cash, Ben and I with the contraband.

In my entire career, this stands out as the simplest undercover transaction I was ever a part of. We could have arrested him on the spot, but since we hadn't planned for that, we let him go – only to be arrested at a later date.

It wasn't long after that Ben and I secured a federal arrest warrant for Welles for the illegal conversion and sale of a machinegun, a 10-year beef. As time came to arrest him, we soon learned that Welles had disappeared off the face of the earth. He had quit his job, moved out of his apartment, and was nowhere to be found. The concerned citizen, who was now a confidential informant, could provide no leads as to Welles' whereabouts.

Ben and I were stumped but continued to "pound the pavement" in search of Welles. Nothing turned up; he was in the wind. At the very least we had kept that one machinegun off the streets, but we were concerned that Welles may have converted many more. We were at a standstill.

It was several months later that Ben and I were contacted by the FBI. We had notified the "Feebs" that should Welles ever be fingerprinted by any police department (all fingerprint cards are sent to the FBI and entered into a national database), we asked to be notified. It just so happened that Welles had been fingerprinted, thus the call from the FBI. However, he had not been arrested; he had re-enlisted in the Army! No wonder we couldn't find him.

After this notification, locating Welles became simple, and we soon learned that he had been sent and stationed at Ft. Leonard Wood near Springfield, Missouri. We coordinated the arrest with the Army's Criminal Investigations Division and soon traveled to Leonard Wood to make the arrest, which went like clockwork. Welles didn't put up any fight, and after the arrest we drove him to the federal building in Springfield for his Initial Appearance before a judge. Ben and I hooked up with some local Springfield ATF agents who took us to meet the judge prior to the hearing; Welles was simply put into federal lock-up in the federal building.

On arriving at the judge's chambers, his secretary instructed us that His Honor was in the basement working out in the gym. One of the Springfield agents knew the judge personally, so we soon went down to the gym to meet him. When we got down to the basement, we found the judge working out on a treadmill. He was an older gentleman, obviously in good shape, and we made small talk with him for several minutes.

One thing, however, I'll never forget about this meeting. While we were talking to the judge, a man appointed by the President of the United States, we noticed something odd. While he was walking briskly on the treadmill, he was also smoking a cigarette! He had an ashtray off to the side which he rested the smoke on occasion, and after I left the meeting I remember laughing my ass off at what I had just witnessed. Smoking a grit while on a treadmill. A District Court Judge appointed by the President.

I thought to myself, "What a stud!" No one was allowed to smoke in a federal building, but this guy couldn't care less. What was anyone going to do? Fire him? You can't fire a federal judge; they are appointed for life. Classic! He was a firm judge too, for he ordered Welles held without bond until he was extradited to Colorado. I guess when you're a judge you can do whatever the hell you want.

Such can also be said for two ostracized students who had an even deadlier agenda.

Chapter XIX

Columbine

On Tuesday, April 20, 1999, at approximately 11:20 A.M., two senior students at Columbine High School in Littleton, Colorado, began a short reign of terror that would shake the world. The two boys, Eric Harris and Dylan Klebold, were loners who constantly and consistently were berated by fellow classmates, but they had a plan to get their revenge. Their place will live in infamy.

The event has obviously been heavily documented for the last decade, so I won't get into all the particulars of what went down that day. I wanted to include this chapter for several reasons: first, I was there during the melee (which I'll detail below); second, like the Los Angeles Riots of 1992, this tragedy shows how poorly and egregiously the ATF brass reacts to such spontaneous combustions; and third, to reiterate how bravely police and investigators handled the scene after all the fireworks had ceased.

I was sitting at a shared computer terminal that morning (which sat in a closet) running criminal histories and/or firearm serial numbers. There were only three of us in the office that day with no secretary. The latter never worked on or around the anniversary of Waco because she was sure our building would be bombed. Pretty funny. My supervisor was in Washington, DC, so we had an acting boss that day. Denver Group II, the Arson & Explosives Group, also had an acting RAC (Resident Agent in Charge) that day.

Usually when the bosses were gone, each group became a ghost town. Translation: agents were out doing whatever, *if* they were even out of bed.

As I sat at the computer a telephone call came into the office. Since our secretary was MIA, I answered the phone. It was from someone in Headquarters. This person asked me if I was watching the television at that time. I thought this was a trick question, for I never watched TV in the office. No one did. I don't think our TV even worked. This person told me that there was a stand-off at a local high school between some armed instigators and students.

I quickly hung up, ran down the hall, and turned on the radio in my office. News was sparse, but a basic description of the incident was given. It was occurring at Columbine High School in Littleton (which actually sits in an unincorporated area of Jefferson County, the county that borders Denver on the west).

I called the other two agents into my office, Russell Brandt and acting-RAC Monte Griffin*. As we listened we knew what we had to do. I don't even think a word was spoken; we just grabbed three rifles and high-tailed it down to Columbine.

I didn't particularly know the area that well, but Brandt did because he lived in Littleton. He knew a route we could take that would get us right onto the school property from the south. As we would learn later this was a good approach and smart plan, for the north and east areas around the school had hundreds of local cops, federal agents, firemen, and families milling about in total chaos.

As we arrived and parked the car, the scene unfolding before us took on a surreal aura. We positioned ourselves behind cover immediately across from the southern parking lot of the school. The time was approximately 12 P.M.

I had never been in such a situation, but my two partners had because they both were ex-military and SWAT team members. When we arrived we asked a local policeman if local SWAT teams were storming the buildings. We were told that a Memorandum of Understanding or similar agreement was in place which stated that should any event of this nature occur in the metropolitan Denver area, Denver PD SWAT would be the team to make the initial entry. This made sense because Denver SWAT was a crack unit that performed sometimes multiple entries each day. The only problem was, we had to wait for them to arrive and formulate their plan, which could take hours.

Intelligence was filtering out of the school (through student cell phones from inside) that students were being executed at random in and around the library which sat on the second floor above the cafeteria. So, there wasn't a minute to spare. Also, apparently one responding officer had already been involved in a shootout with one or more of the assailants.

Being that it was lunchtime at the school, kids were running out in our direction like a stampede. As I watched these kids running for their lives, I soon noticed that many were bleeding but were still able to escape. Brandt, Griffin, and I quickly came to the conclusion that whoever was doing the shooting inside obviously didn't have any heavy firepower like AK-47's or automatic rifles. If that had been the case, *no* children would have been escaping – at least not on foot or with all limbs attached. The three of us looked at each other, racked our rifles into fire mode, and decided to make some sort of effort to approach the scene through the south parking lot. No word had to be uttered; we knew what had to be done. Besides, that's what we were being paid to do.

At almost the instant we had decided to get involved, Griffin received a call on his cell phone from the Assistant Special Agent in Charge (ASAC) of the Phoenix Field Division. The ASAC, Joseph Evans*, was screaming at Griffin on the other end. Evans made his instructions clear: we, or any responding agents would not engage the assailants. The three of us looked at each other in bewilderment.

I grabbed the phone from Griffin and gave Evans our assessment of the scene and the number of survivors who were escaping. Evans remained adamant: we would not engage, and if we went against these orders then there would be hell to pay. Now, I'm not saying that the three of us would have been able to do anything to save any lives; odds are we probably wouldn't have (supported later by the actual time frame of the incident). Nonetheless, our adrenaline was pumping. In addition, we had rifles and bullet proof vests, and if anything we might be able to approach and maybe do something. There was excellent cover adjacent the cafeteria, for it was a student parking lot full of cars. It also gave a great vantage point of the library.

Evans would have no part of it; we were ordered to stand down and that was the end of it.

As we would learn later, the two assailants would end their barrage in the coming minutes (around 12:15 P.M.) by committing suicide in the library. After nearly an hour they had left 12 students and a teacher dead, as well as wounding over 20 additional students.

Harris and Klebold had gotten their sweet revenge for all the bullying they had received.

The aftermath was as chaotic as the incident itself. By the time we walked to the north end of the school, there had to be over 1000 cops and emergency personnel milling around looking for answers. Of course, no one had any. Also, other ATF agents had begun to arrive from the Arson & Explosives Group. These agents had driven out in our bomb truck because intelligence was relayed saying that the assailants also had brought improvised explosive devices (IEDs) into the cafeteria.

I don't know how long it took, but I believe it was several hours later that the scene was finally declared Code 4, or safe to conduct follow-up investigation, by entering SWAT teams. The scene inside the cafeteria and library was gruesome. Several IEDs were in plain view and apparently had failed to detonate. The cafeteria was also under four inches of water because all the sprinklers had been activated. Since it had been lunchtime, the cafeteria was also littered with hundreds of backpacks. Which backpack(s) may have contained additional IEDs was anyone's guess. In addition, the south parking lot had a least a hundred cars parked in it.

In all we knew it would be a long day and night, for each backpack and car would have to be inspected for IEDs. One such device was indeed found in one of the assailant's cars in the south lot. It would take more than a day to clear all the backpacks and cars, and this was done by local bomb squad cops as well as ATF agents from the Arson & Explosives Group. I made a habit of staying away from explosives because a friend of mine had been killed trying to dismantle a bomb several years earlier. That was a job for the experts, but even that could be a coin flip at times. My friend had been one of ATF's most respected bomb-handling agents. Sometimes it didn't matter how qualified you were; some criminals were always a step ahead of law enforcement.

Just ask any soldier who toured in the Middle East.

As days progressed details of the two assailants began to emerge. ATF had primary jurisdiction over the case, though every agency in the area offered its assistance. There's an amusing aside to this fact which occurred in the ensuing days after the massacre. ASAC Evans had sent his two best Arson & Explosives investigators in Phoenix to participate in the subsequent investigation. One of the agents was a guy named Arthur Knight*.

I'd known Knight for many years, and after he arrived in Denver he was present at one of the first briefings. The briefing was chaired by an FBI supervisor or SAIC, and after giving his talk he asked if there were any questions to be voiced by any of the attendees. What happened next was classic Knight. I think he was the only one who raised his hand, and when called upon he looked the FBI SAIC in the eye and uttered the following question, "Why are *you* here?" Knight was obviously making it known to all participants that ATF was in charge, not the FBI.

I lowered my head and tried to control my laughter. You could have heard a pin drop in that room. I don't remember the outcome of this confrontation but I do know one thing – ASAC Evans had Knight on a plane back to Phoenix that very afternoon. Evans nearly went through the roof! Then again, he usually did over just about anything.

Intelligence began to flow like the Colorado River. We soon learned that a girl had purchased several firearms for Harris and Klebold, and that another individual named Mark Manes had purchased one of the pistols found at the scene. Griffin became case agent on the case and Denver Group I, our group, would handle all investigation into the gun side of the case. Denver Group II would handle the explosives end.

Griffin and I soon got on to Manes and arrested him in a car stop several days later after conducting surveillance on him. We had no directions to arrest, only to watch Manes, but we didn't give a shit. We hooked him anyway. Manes would eventually receive a substantial sentence in state court – six to eight years I believe. Not a bad hit for someone who didn't even have a criminal record.

The ensuing investigation gained worldwide notoriety and was under intense scrutiny from day one. ATF Denver did work the case well – which was a rarity – and many were awarded cash awards after the case had been adjudicated. Griffin's work was notably outstanding, and my respect for Brandt increased tremendously even after all the footdragging I had experienced in the Georgia Pawn case. My award was minimal, which was fine, for I was only a secondary player in the whole thing. Plus, I didn't ask for one. Not surprisingly, most of ASAC Evans' pet agents received more money than others who worked just as hard, if not harder, on the case – including Griffen. Such is the way of ATF.

I want to end this chapter by stating that despite all the chaos, every law enforcement officer present that day had one mission: to end the massacre as quickly as possible. The presence of so many jurisdictions, and the fact that the scene was utter bedlam, precluded any quicker response, but that does not erase the fact that all responding personnel, emergency crews included, acted bravely and professionally. A witch hunt soon followed trying to lay blame on just about everyone, and this was wrong. There was no way anyone could have been prepared for what transpired that day.

Yet, lessons were learned and tactics subsequently put in place to hopefully preclude any such tragedy from happening in the future.

Hats off to every man and woman who was there that day and who would assist in the subsequent investigations.

More importantly, my prayers go out to the families and students who will be scarred for life because of two idiotic teens who felt it was okay to kill defenseless human beings to make a point. May they rot in hell.

Unbeknownst to me or anyone during the months of follow-up investigation, a ball was being set in motion for me to rot in hell as well, though my soon-to-be-occupied Hades usually never exceeded 120 degrees Fahrenheit.

Chapter XX

ATF Agent Drive-By: Act II

This incident was a little more coordinated than the first – some aforethought had been undertaken. The setting for this shooting was very different from the first: this time I found myself no longer in an urban environment, but rather in a rural setting – where the stars seemed to reach down and touch the prairie and where one's nearest neighbor would normally be several miles away. On paper probably the perfect place for such a crime, but some subtle planning had to be undertaken.

The background of the story is as follows: I had a confidential informant who was providing intelligence about local criminals in the area. It so happened the main criminals were one big family, similar to the Rojo clan in the Clint Eastwood classic *A Fistful of Dollars*. It was a farming community/small town environment where everyone knew everybody, and it didn't take long for the family, who I'll call the Baxters*, to realize who was spilling the beans about their illicit enterprises – activities ranging from narcotics trafficking, firearms violations, extortion, witness tampering, and anything else one could imagine.

One day I received a call from my informant that he/she had been shot at by a couple members of this family on an afternoon as he/she was tending crops. He/she wasn't sure if the two Baxters had been deliberately shooting at him/her, or whether or not they were just firing into the air to send a message. Whatever the intention, the message had been delivered – air mail if you will.

My informant was scared for his/her life (most are, though I felt this occurrence added a little more exigency and panic to the situation). I soon vehemently contacted several of the Baxters, and though speaking in a roundabout way, I made it clear that making any trouble in town or elsewhere, would only make me come down on them hard. I had no problem laying these cards, for the Baxters, through the omnipresent hayseed grapevine, knew that the Feds were poking around their territory. I couldn't make the city limits without news of my arrival being the talk of the town. Anyway, I made my point and soon went on my way.

For a while.

Since we were working in conjunction with the local police who were friends of mine, I had no problem inquiring one late night whether or not there'd be local police or troopers working outside of town into the dead of night. I was told that the area in which I was interested had no active police coverage from about midnight until daybreak. An officer could be called at all hours of the night, but he would have to be roused out of bed to make any kind of response.

That was all I needed to hear.

This time I would need an accomplice, and after procuring one we set out in his/her large sedan and made haste into the vast countryside. It was roughly 3 A.M., maybe later. Unlike my first drive-by experience, this time I sat in the back of the vehicle and with a much more powerful weapon. I also knew which individual house I was looking for; it was the most accessible and easiest from which to make a safe getaway. I told my driver exactly where to go, what speed to drive, and exactly which route to take afterwards.

To this day I'm unclear whether or not my accomplice knew exactly what I was up to, but as I took my shotgun out of its case and racked that first shell into the chamber, there could be no guessing at that point.

It wasn't long before the targeted farmhouse came into view, and as we passed it I fired every round in that shotgun at my prey. Fittingly, all expended casings fell in the back seat or on my lap (leaving no evidence).

As soon as the fireworks had ended, the car's engine quickly growled to the tune of a high-octane getaway in the night. Again I felt the feeling of satisfaction, though this incident had more of a purpose than the last, for I felt completely justified. This time I knew no one could be killed, due to the spray, but I also knew that another more important message had been delivered.

My informant was never screwed with again.

Chapter XXI

Exile Pt. II: Banishment to the Desk

Two months before the Columbine massacre I attended a gang conference in Nashville, Tennessee. It was the fourth such conference I had attended in six years (I had been to three in Anaheim), and I always gleaned as much information from these gatherings as possible. Thankfully ATF had footed the bill for my frequent attendances, and I think the money was well spent.

If only the Nashville trip had been denied, for it would mark the beginning of the end for me as an ATF agent.

Before attending the conference on a Monday I elected to spend time the preceding weekend with a childhood friend from high school who lived in Louisville, Kentucky. Louisville was approximately 280 miles north of Nashville, so on Friday I flew into Nashville, rented a car (with my own money), and drove north to spend the weekend with my friend Chef*. I hadn't seen Chef in nearly six years, so I looked forward to the visit. I arrived in Louisville on Friday night and spent an uneventful evening just shooting the shit and making up for the previous six years.

The next morning Chef arranged a little road trip with a friend of his named Wild Phil*. Wild Phil was the quintessential redneck. He claimed to be a Vietnam veteran, had a long white beard, and as Chef would tell me before the introduction, hated the government with a passion. I didn't think much of the latter fact, being that most people don't like the government, but I nonetheless asked Chef to keep my true identity a secret.

Sometime on Saturday morning we picked up Wild Phil. We were in Chef's car, and after picking up Phil we drove south to the town of Muldraugh which sits adjacent to the more famous township of Ft. Knox.

The drive south was only about thirty minutes, but in that short span of time I learned quite a bit about Wild Phil. Apparently he had been in Vietnam, had 150 confirmed kills while on tour (bullshit probably), and interestingly he also grew marijuana and made in upwards of $100,000 per year from its illegal cultivation. This I *knew* was bullshit because the house he was living in was an absolute shithole; you could barely walk in the place. I'd been in crack dens more habitable. If Phil had made that kind of money off the "hippie lettuce," then he obviously invested the proceeds elsewhere.

I also had the pleasure of listening to Phil spout out how he despised the federal government and would do anything in his power to flip the bird to Uncle Sam, especially the DEA. The story was fairly humorous and ridiculous, but I kept my mouth shut nonetheless.

While driving into Muldraugh, Chef decided to visit a friend who lived there. When we arrived he pulled his car in front of a single-wide trailer, parked, and walked up to the front door. I stayed in the vehicle. In the meantime, Wild Phil decided it would be a good idea to get out and urinate in the middle of the street. Though I didn't know it at the time, he had been drinking since the break of dawn and was fairly obliterated. I wasn't the only one who saw this indiscreet display in the street, for a neighbor also witnessed it.

That citizen would eventually call the police.

Chef met with his acquaintance for about ten minutes, and we were soon on our way back to Louisville – this time with me behind the wheel. As I drove north up Highway 31W, I soon noticed a police car behind me with its lights on. I quickly pulled over and exited the car to meet with the officer, who was a Kentucky State Patrolman. As soon as I met the officer I identified myself (out of sight of my two passengers) and I told him that I would fully cooperate. I told him I was attending a gang conference in Nashville the following week and was only visiting a childhood friend.

But I also asked him a favor. I asked him not to divulge my true identity to Wild Phil (who I pointed out) because of Phil's anti-government beliefs and overall questionable demeanor. The officer was cordial and said he wouldn't say anything. I thanked him and inquired about the stop.

He told me that someone in Muldraugh had called the police because someone in our vehicle had been urinating in the street. I told the officer that had been Phil (which I think he already knew), and if he wanted to take Phil to jail or cite him, then be my guest.

At about this time another police car drove up and parked. This car belonged to a Muldraugh cop, and as it turned out, it was the Chief of Police. I introduced myself to him and asked the same favor of him, and he complied. What I didn't know at the time was that the Muldraugh chief and Wild Phil had a history; this would come into play later.

Both officers advised me of the reason for the stop and agreed to let me go, but not before simulating a breathalyzer test. Now, I hadn't been drinking (it was only 11 A.M.), but I obliged; no one was arrested or cited, and I was just advised to drive back to Louisville and get rid of Wild Phil. No problem I said. After that we were on our way.

Little did I know the repercussions this five minute encounter would entail.

I finished up my weekend with Chef (I stayed the hell away from Wild Phil) and drove back to Nashville Monday morning. The conference began on Tuesday and would proceed until Thursday. That Tuesday morning I received a phone call from an agent friend of mine from the Kansas City Field Division. His name was Claude*.

I hadn't spoken to Claude for several years, so I thought it odd he would be calling me, especially at that hour of the morning. What he told me gave me a huge head's-up. Claude said that he had been in Louisville over the weekend and had been in the Louisville Division office. While there he had overheard details about my traffic stop on Saturday. Claude stated that the Louisville brass had been called by the Muldraugh Chief of Police who related the traffic stop in entirely different terms.

Apparently he had told the Louisville Special Agent in Charge (SAC) that he had stopped an ATF agent over the weekend who had used his position and badge to get out of a ticket or DUI. Moreover, the Chief told the SAC that I had told him (the Chief) that I was working undercover and that it would be best for him to let me go so as not to jeopardize a federal enforcement operation. Complete and utter bullshit!

The first thing ATF trains its undercover agents in (and I had been to Advanced Undercover School) is to never carry credentials while in an undercover capacity. Nothing worse than an undercover agent pulling out his wallet and inadvertently showing his badge. Second, an undercover agent is to be armed with a firearm at all times while in an undercover role. This is right out of the ATF directives. The day of the traffic stop (a Saturday no less) I had my credentials on me as well as no firearm. Not a good operating procedure if one is in an undercover role. Nonetheless, the Muldraugh Chief said that I had told him I was working undercover. It also just so happened that there was an Internal

Affairs (IA) agent in the Louisville Field Division office that weekend. The guy, Dom Wopat*, would figure in my life for the next several years – and he would have a serious axe to grind.

That Tuesday morning, after Claude's call, I received a call from my boss back in Denver. He told me that the ASAC in Phoenix, Joseph Evans*, had called him in a furor. ASAC Evans apparently had been contacted by the Louisville Field Division SAC regarding the traffic stop and the story told to him by the Muldraugh Chief of Police. ASAC Evans wanted answers, and since shit filters downhill, I subsequently received the call from my boss. I related to him the real story, and he told me he would take care of relaying the information back to Phoenix. I thought that was the end of it.

Boy, was I wrong!

The following week after arriving back in Denver, I was told by my boss that Internal Affairs was coming to Denver in the ensuing weeks to interview me about the traffic stop. This interview was to take place after everyone involved (i.e., in Kentucky) had already been interviewed, so, my session took place two or three weeks later. The IA investigator coming to Colorado was none other than Dom Wopat.

The day Wopat arrived and began interviewing me I knew I was in hot water. I had dealt with IA many times in the past, so I knew the SOP. Regardless, Wopat had his own operating procedure. He treated me like a criminal the minute he introduced himself, and after conducting his interview with me, he handed me a stack of blank paper and instructed me to go to my office and write a statement.

This was definitely out of character. Usually after the initial interview, the IA investigator would sit down with the agent and both would compose the agent statement together. Wopat would have none of that; he only handed me the affidavit forms and ordered me to go complete my statement of the incident.

The first thing I did when I got back to my desk was email several friends of mine, some who had been in IA. I was given Wopat's entire history, which was basically that he had been a boob his whole career but now was a headhunter for Internal Affairs, viz., all agents were guilty until proven otherwise – in complete contrast to every other IA investigator I had dealt with over the years. I knew I had to make my statement truthful (there were times in the past where I had definitely been guilty by omission of key facts) because my career was now on the line – and this time for something I didn't do.

I must have spent four to five hours completing my affidavit. Every thirty minutes or so Wopat would come into my office and ask me if I had finished. He was rushing me to be sure, but I took my sweet time in making my statement truthful and full of the facts. Plus, I wanted to fuck with him for treating me unprofessionally and like a criminal.

When I finally finished I walked down the hall and handed the statement to Wopat. Without even reading it, he just stuffed it in his briefcase and left the office. Usually an IA investigator would read over the affidavit to make sure every subject had been touched upon, but Wopat didn't care. He just left, and as quickly as he appeared, he was in the wind.

I would never see him again, but his legacy would take center stage in my ordeal.

When Internal Affairs conducts an investigation, it is (at least on paper) a fact-finding entity. After the full investigation is conducted, a completed report is sent to a disciplinary panel (called the Professional Review Board) to render punishment to the agent in question. Arriving at this decision can take anywhere from six months to several years. Such run the gears of justice. I didn't really care how long it took, for I was sure I'd be cleared. As a result, I just continued working in the field as I always had.

But then the roof caved in.

In December 1999, after nearly eight months, the Professional Review Board (PRB) rendered its decision: dismissal from the Bureau! I was flabbergasted to say the least, but knowing how bloodthirsty Wopat had been, the resulting sentence didn't necessarily surprise me.

When the PRB renders its decision, it isn't necessarily final. The agent can then appeal the sentence, whereupon the ultimate deciding official becomes the SAC of the respective field division. Though the SAC of the Phoenix Field Division was a friend of mine, I took no chances. I hired an attorney on the spot (which cost me plenty), and the bulk of 2000 was spent by my attorney and me doing our own investigation, the results of which we would produce to the SAC at a later date. Everyone was re-interviewed in the case, and I even took a polygraph examination to refute the claims. I passed with flying colors (of course), and the examiner even told me it was the best score he'd ever seen on a lie-detector test. During our investigation we also learned that the Muldraugh Chief and Wild Phil had a long history, none of which was good. This, I knew, would prove to be good fodder to include in the ultimate report submitted to the SAC.

A date was set for my attorney and me to meet with the SAC. We all met in my attorney's office, and the SAC pretty much just listened and told us he would render his decision in the near future. I felt confident I would be cleared, though I had to prepare for just about anything. Unfortunately, I couldn't prepare for what was to happen behind closed doors and without my knowing.

I learned later that the Phoenix SAC's final recommendation was that I receive no punishment and be completely cleared of any wrongdoing. ATF Headquarters didn't like this decision however, and unbeknownst to me at the time, decided to take the final decision authority away from the SAC and bump it up to the next level, that is, to the SAC's boss in Washington, DC. This gentlemen, like Wopat, was also known as a headhunter. I then knew I was in deeper shit. I even began to look for another job.

The shit soon began to mount on another front. The United States Attorney's Office (USAO) in Denver soon got wind of the vortex whirling around me. An Assistant US Attorney had requested a copy of my personnel file to turn over to the defense in a case of mine – not an uncommon occurrence. Unfortunately, the documents sent to the AUSA contained the whole Kentucky incident – despite the fact that the case was still ongoing. As a result, the USAO held many meetings about me (without me present) and came to the decision to not prosecute any case that I was involved in – at least not until the final decision was rendered regarding the Kentucky incident. It was Los Angeles all over again.

As I said in a previous chapter, the USAO thinks about itself first, despite the individual in question. I was one of the favorite agents of the Denver USAO, with whom I had enjoyed a great working relationship for nearly seven years, but when it came right down to it, it suddenly wanted nothing to do with me. Again I was persona non grata and cast to the wolves.

As fate would have it, the SAC's boss who was to decide my fate was soon promoted to another position (where he would be buried for the remainder of his inauspicious career) and replaced by another person. The stars could not have been any more in alignment, for the latter individual had been my SAC when I was in the Kansas City Field Division. He had always been good to me, and though I couldn't predict how he would rule, I at least knew he'd be fair. I still however continued looking for another occupation.

In the meantime and for the bulk of 2001, I was placed on Administrative Leave. Admin Leave, as it is called, meant you were to stay at home and not come into the office. You remained on pay status, but the feeling and embarrassment of being on Admin Leave is immeasurable. I never knew when I would get that phone call telling me of the ultimate decision, but I can assure you that every time the phone rang I got a nauseous feeling throughout my body. The wait was excruciating.

That call came about eight months later.

I still get butterflies in my stomach when I talk about it. I was told that I was ultimately to serve a 45-day suspension for the incident. The initial charge of Making False Statements to a Law Enforcement Officer were not sustained, though a new charge was added, that is, Embarrassing the Bureau. If I haven't talked about it already, the latter charge is the catch-all of charges – it can basically be attributed to any agent who is investigated, but it is not a fire-able offense. I took the forty-five in stride – I even traveled to the Caribbean – and sometime in the fall of 2001, I returned to work.

But the saga, I'm sad to say, wasn't over.

As I would soon learn, despite the ultimate ruling, the Denver USAO would still have nothing to do with me. Hell, there were ATF agents on the job that had committed felonies who continued to testify in federal court, but the Denver USAO still thought I was a pariah. Though I could never prove it, it became the belief of many, including me, that someone in ATF Headquarters had reached out to the United States Attorney in Denver with some *suggestions* for dealing with me. I've never been a conspiracy theorist, but I wouldn't put anything past the brass in DC.

Hell had finally come to *my* house.

It was a Friday night, the weekend before I was to return to work in Denver the following Monday morning. I received a call from a fellow Denver agent who told me some shocking news. This individual told me that an announcement had come across the ATF wire that afternoon (Friday) announcing that I had been transferred to the Phoenix Field Division office in Phoenix, and that I was to become a Senior Operations Officer. In other words, I was off the street. Not only that, I was to be jettisoned from Colorado, the state where I had enjoyed the most success of my career as a federal agent. I was to be presented with this news on Monday morning, but again I had been tipped off. It's good to have friends in the right places.

Administration. A desk job. This was ATF Headquarters' final "fuck you" and way of telling me that even though I had dodged another bullet, this was my ultimate punishment. Another lesson in the way of how ATF treated its troops and better agents, for you see, it was never the slacker or slug agents that got in trouble. It was always the working agents. There's an old phrase: work hard, play hard, fall hard. I was the poster child of that worn-out adage. I most certainly could have initiated a lawsuit at this time (I was urged to by many), but like all previous times, I decided to take my punishment and move forward.

I was given three months to get my affairs in order in Denver before I would report to duty in Phoenix on January 2, 2002. The only affair I had to take care of was taken care of for me. My live-in girlfriend at the time, my fiancée, told me that she would not be accompanying me to Phoenix. Just as being reassigned to Denver had broken up my marriage for good, so did my move to the Valley of the Sun break up the former relationship forever. It was hard to swallow, but I had to go. I had a young son who lived in California who was to enter college in the near future, so I couldn't jeopardize his future because of my past.

I remember the night I left. It was heart-wrenching. At the time my ex-fiancée could only cry and see me off. It was a bitter cold December night, and after making that initial climb into the Rocky Mountains, I knew my life was taking a serious turn. For the better or worse could only be speculated.

I decided to make the best of it. Besides and on the upside, I was now closer to my son.

Even better, I would also soon be co-piloting the Phoenix Field Division ship – and in a way management could never have foreseen.

Chapter XXII

Soup

On May 29, 1998, a water truck/tanker was stolen in the vicinity of Durango, Colorado, and a radio call soon went out alerting all police agencies in the Four Corners region (CO, UT, NM, and AZ) to the theft.

Sometime after, Cortez (CO) Police Department Officer Dale Claxton saw a truck matching the description in Cortez. He turned on his police lights and pulled the suspect vehicle over; in the cab of the truck were three individuals. Before Claxton could even exit his police car he was riddled with automatic weapons fire from one or more of the occupants, leaving him dead before he could even blink. The truck quickly left the scene of the murder.

Shortly thereafter, the three suspects dumped the water truck and carjacked a flatbed pickup truck. The newly-stolen vehicle then began driving westbound in the direction of southeastern Utah. Two of the suspects rode in the front cab while the third stood in the back with a fully-automatic rifle.

Local police vehicles soon arrived and gave chase to the flatbed. This was right out of a Hollywood movie. Speeds were well over the speed limit, but this didn't stop the lone gunman in the back of the truck from spraying all pursuing vehicles with weapon's fire. Before the chase ended nine police cars were damaged and several officers wounded.

The truck sped towards Utah and soon crossed the state line into Hovenweep National Monument. Hovenweep, meaning "deserted valley" to the local Piute and Ute Indians, was a familiar playground for the three suspects. All were young white males, in their early twenties, and they liked to play simulated war games in that desolate part of southeastern Utah. They were also survivalists, and were known to have stashed many provisions in the unpopulated area, everything from canned foods, to clothing, to ammunition, to just about everything. This was their home away from home, and they knew they would have the upper hand dealing with any kind of police pursuit.

After getting into Hovenweep and shooting at just about everyone, the three assailants finally dumped the stolen flatbed in a ditch; they also attempted to camouflage the vehicle from any aerial support they knew was soon to arrive. Once out of the truck (opinions differ) one thing was for certain, these guys were well armed and were now luring all responding officers into their second home. It was *Rambo* to the nth degree, only now there were three to contend with.

The manhunt progressed for a week, and it wasn't until June 4 that one of the suspects was found and cornered. He put up a good fight, including shooting a San Juan County (UT) deputy from 400 yards. As the gauntlet tightened, the fugitive would take his own life with his Glock pistol. It was an interesting death scene because the suspect, Robert Mason, was wearing a ballistic helmet at the time of "swallowing" his gun. When the helmet was removed, all that was left was "brain salad."

The real interesting thing was in that week's time, Mason had hiked over twenty miles and with full gear, provisions which included multiple pipe bombs, two ballistic vests, pistol, a rifle, as well as food and other wares. The most serious wound to the boy's body, minus the self-inflicted gunshot, was a terrible case of chafed upper thighs. Had he not been cornered, many wondered if he wouldn't have escaped altogether. It was what all three commonly trained for. Their war game was coming to fruition, and many of us were beginning to ask if these guys were living out some kind of demented combat fantasy.

I became involved in the case soon after the Mason death. Why I responded to this incident, I still don't know because I was from the Denver office, and the Four Corners area was in the realm of the Colorado Springs Field Office. Never one to turn down an assignment, I made the seven-hour, 400 mile journey to Cortez; I was told to pack a bag for an indefinite time – something I had become very good at.

Cortez, Colorado, is a small town of about 8000 people and is known as a staging location for tourists wishing to visit nearby Mesa Verde National Monument, Lake Powell, and the Four Corners. What I found the afternoon of my arrival was a town in utter panic. By now all the perpetrators had been identified, and their stories weren't very appealing. All were survivalist types who amassed weapons, hated the government, and had no problem advertising their hatred to the local residents. Most brushed them off as big-talking gun freaks, but after the Claxton murder townspeople were locking their doors at night.

I would have as well.

By the time of my arrival a command post had been set up at the Cortez PD by the FBI and many other federal, state, and local agencies. The FBI was in charge, and the coordination and cooperation among all was very good. The plan was this: the flatbed truck had been found; Mason had been found and eliminated (after a 20-mile trek!); and the other two, Jason McVean and Alan Pilon, were still at large in the Hovenweep wilderness. The plan was to walk the canyons, do helicopter flyovers, bring in bloodhounds, everything.

What I had signed on for I would soon learn.

It was now June and the mercury was hovering in the 100 degree neighborhood. Knowing that I'd be walking the canyons, I dressed accordingly, though I did pack a lot of gear. Intelligence stated that all three suspects were adept marksmen, and Mason had exhibited that fact when he shot a sheriff's deputy at four hundred yards. The other two were supposed to be better shots – especially McVean who was the leader of the crew.

I remember driving out to Hovenweep with two FBI agents, good guys, in an air-conditioned SUV, but when we got to the flatbed truck location, it was time to disembark. And it was hot. The topography and terrain resembled the Grand Canyon, though not as vast and deep. We would be walking canyons and creek droughts with mesas towering 400 feet above us on each side. I had my .223 Colt AR-15 rifle, but I knew I was a sitting duck walking this wilderness. Any good sniper could have taken me out, and from up to 1000 yards. It was guerilla warfare at its finest.

And it was the most scared I'd ever been as an ATF agent. I just waited for that final shot.

My initial job was to provide cover (lol) to a cadaver dog that was sniffing around the area. I'd worked with narcotics and bomb dogs, but never with a dog that keyed on dead carcasses. He was a big floppy-eared bloodhound, something you'd expect to see in a cartoon. But the dog was thorough. Why we had a cadaver dog out there threw me, because odds were good that the suspects were very much alive and running from the cops. *Hopefully* running. If they were staging an ambush, I was a dead man and I knew it.

Being that it was so hot, the dog could only work for 30-45 minutes. He then needed to rest, rehydrate, and whatever else. For the grunts like me there was no rest. We began walking this one canyon, and my eyes were all over the place. I surveyed mesa tops, outcroppings, potential caves, any place where these fucks could have hidden. In all it was a useless hunt, for the crooks could have been anywhere and hopefully many miles away. Working this slowly with the dogs brought tedium to a new level, but it was the best we could do on the ground. Hopefully, aerial reconnaissance would prove better.

This went on for a week.

After finding nothing I soon returned to Denver and began compiling a federal case against the surviving two suspects McVean and Pilon. They would subsequently be indicted and federal warrants issued for their arrest. Once in the system, if one or both of these guys were to be picked up anywhere in the world, then I would be notified.

Several posses continued searching the desert canyons of southeastern Utah, including many bounty hunters, but McVean and Pilon were in the wind. Literally.

Halloween 1999, over a year later, I was walking down the hall to give testimony before the Grand Jury in regards to the McVean-Pilon case. The United States Attorney's Office (USAO) was charging the two with multiple federal firearms and explosives violations, all the way up to the capital offense of Claxton's murder I believe.

I proudly walked the halls of the Federal Building that morning because I wanted to see those two maniacs fry.

As I sat in the Grand Jury waiting room I received a telephone call from one of the Assistant United States Attorneys (AUSAs) on the case. Apparently the remains of one of the two fugitives had been found – and not far from where I had walked the canyon a year before. It was Alan Pilon, who was known to have a bad leg, and his body lay under some bushes. When I asked the AUSA what the body looked like, he said "soup." Adjacent the morass were bombs, guns, vests, etc. Just like Mason.

Two down, one to go. As a result, only McVean was indicted that day, though it may have been another day since the indictment had to be rewritten excluding Pilon's name.

In June 2007 Jason McVean's remains were found in Utah with the same array of toys: guns, vests, bombs, ammo, supplies, etc. The ending leaves little solace for the many who worked that case, especially those of us who walked the canyons in 100-degree heat. My college baseball coach always said, "Never give-in to the elements." I never forgot that phrase, and though it was phrased for the athletic realm, I referred to that maxim many times in my professional career, especially in Colorado. Thanks Coach, you had a hand in making me a man.

And Dale Claxton, your name will never be forgotten.

This case will always remain open in my mind because we (the investigators) could never identify why the three survivalists wanted a water truck in the beginning. Stealing that vehicle was a major heist – not just measured in balls but also in advertisement. They weren't going to go far without being recognized. So, why the water truck? Some thought they were planning a robbery of a local Indian casino, for there was captured footage of the suspects scoping out such an establishment. But still, why the water truck? This enigma I'll take to my grave, but I do know one thing: all three got what they deserved.

Part Three

Valley

of the

Sun

The federal government is one big Ponzi scheme.
- Bernie Madoff

Chapter XXIII

Nine Eleven

On the morning of September 11, 2001, four jets took off from Boston, Newark, and Washington, DC in route to the west coast. Two planes subsequently crashed into the World Trade Center in Manhattan, one into the Pentagon, and one into a field in Pennsylvania. Nearly three thousand people died, and the history of our nation was forever changed. Much has been chronicled about this disaster, so I won't recount all the facts, speculations, and conspiracy theories. Like the JFK assassination, every American will remember where he/she was that day; I am no exception.

On that fateful morning I was camping with my twelve year-old son in the Santa Monica Mountains west of Los Angeles. I was serving a 45-day suspension that had been tacked on to nearly seven months of paid administrative leave stemming from the Kentucky incident (see Chapter XXI).

We awoke at around 8 A.M. PDT, or 11 EDT – a full two hours after the disasters. My son and I were well into the outback and were the only people for probably ten square miles. As was standard procedure on all night hikes, I had brought a boom box to play music and keep any critters away (or humans). For some reason that morning I decided to switch over from cassette mode to radio. I state this fact because it was a rarity; I almost never played the radio on hikes. Cassettes or CDs were always the norm, but on that morning I elected to play the radio. I still don't know why.

Since we were in the mountains reception wasn't that great, and the Howard Stern show became the only option. I usually wouldn't listen to Stern with my young son around, but that morning it was the best station I could locate, even though it kept fading in and out.

Over the next hour or so of hiking to our car, we kept getting bits and pieces of information of what had happened on the east coast. The Stern show had become a local (though syndicated) newscast, and by the time we got to the car we had learned that something terrible had happened. We didn't know much – only that some airplanes had crashed into the World Trade Center and Pentagon. My hat goes off to the Stern broadcast and the way its normally ribald format dealt seriously with the tragedy. It was intense radio.

It was nearly 11 A.M. PDT (2 EDT), after arriving at a friend's house and turning on the television, that my son and I got a clearer picture of what had happened that morning. I was at a loss for words – as I'm sure every person on the planet was – yet suddenly I became aware and thankful that my young son was with me that day. I didn't see him that much; he lived in San Diego and I in Denver, but to this day I know he was by my side for a reason, for he had many questions that I answered or attempted to answer. I can only thank the One Above for putting us together that morning.

My father, I learned later, was in the air that morning on a flight from Wichita to Los Angeles when the attacks occurred. His plane had just taken off, and as soon as word reached the cockpit of what was transpiring, the pilot got on the intercom and told his passengers, "Ladies and gentlemen, we are returning to Wichita, for America is under attack." That's all he said as the plane made a U-turn and returned to Wichita. If it wasn't for the fact that my dad had a friend who owned a used car lot in Wichita, he would have been stranded in Kansas for nearly a week. Thousands of travelers that week would not be so lucky.

In terms of investigation, ATF teamed up with the FBI in every U.S. city and followed leads meted out from Washington, DC. I returned to work soon after 9/11 and performed shifts at the newly-formed Joint Terrorism Task Force in Denver. I don't remember anything significant in terms of investigation, so I can only assume Colorado wasn't directly connected to the attacks or any leads in any substantial way. I may be wrong, though I wasn't privy to any.

I do know that many ATF agents on the east coast worked their butts off on subsequent investigations. Many in New York and Washington had even been in or around the Ground Zeros, and many suffer severe and chronic health problems to this day. This short chapter is dedicated to the men and women who did all they could to assist the victims that day. Your contribution to history is immeasurable. Any courage I may have exhibited during my career pales in comparison to your endeavors. Peace be with you all.

An interesting by-product of 9/11 occurred in 2002 when the Department of Homeland Security was established, triggering an overall restructuring of government agencies. ATF went from the Department of Treasury to the Justice Department, which seemed the right place to be considering its mission. However, no one foresaw what was to evolve over the ensuing years, that is, ATF's drop in prestige, resources, and clout. At Treasury ATF agents were the prodigal sons of the department – elite; at Justice, they became the fourth or even fifth rung on the departmental ladder, behind the FBI, DEA, the United States Attorney's Office, even the US Marshal's Service. This restructuring left ATF with little or no leverage in the federal arena, examples of which would only come to the forefront at the end of the decade. This will be detailed later.

Chapter XXIV

Administration

I didn't know what to expect that first day in Phoenix. I didn't even know how to dress, for I had never even seen a Senior Operations Officer. I think I wore a tie (something I never did unless I had court), and I'm sure I looked like a fish out of water.

Luckily I was met by a glorious staff. Secretaries in ATF – all staff, for that matter – never get the recognition they deserve. Most are treated like garbage by their bosses, who seem to think that since these folks are on a lower pay scale, they are inferior. As I said in the first chapter of this book, I always tried to treat the staff professionally and deferentially. They are the backbone of any federal agency, but especially ATF.

I quickly made friends with all sorts of people. I shared an office with two other operations officers and I just tried to fit in as quickly as possible. My first-line boss (the person I directly reported to) was a woman from the Compliance/Regulatory side of the ATF house who was the Division Operations Officer (DOO). She was always nice to me, and I treated her accordingly. She explained to me that first day what my duties would be and how to go about them.

The ultimate boss of the Phoenix Field Division was another story.

Special Agent in Charge (SAC) Georgia McKay* was legendary around the Bureau – and *not* in a good way. She had been an Assistant Special Agent in Charge (ASAC) in Los Angeles after I had left, but my friends there kept me well informed about her over the years. In LA she was dubbed "The Magistrate," because even after a federal judge had signed a search/arrest warrant for true probable cause, McKay had to read the affidavit and have the final authority on whether or not probable cause did in fact exist and, consequently, whether or not the operation would go forward. She shot down several warrants that had been authorized by federal judges – people appointed by the President of the United States – only because she felt that the affidavits were weak.

And if she didn't like you, then you felt her wrath even more.

She was also known as a big-time boozer, and agents in Los Angeles contemplated following her home at night after she'd been out on a bender in order to report her to the local cops to have her arrested. This strategy never worked however.

We thought about performing the same type of surveillance on her in Phoenix, but this proved impossible for she rarely parked her government car in the assigned ATF lot. Where her car really was, no one ever knew. Maybe she took the bus home; I don't know. In other words, she wasn't as stupid as many thought.

I was scheduled to meet with SAC McKay my first day in the office. Inside, I was quite indignant about being transferred to Phoenix, especially without any input on my part, but I never let her know it. I kissed her ass like I would any SAC; I even thanked her for the new opportunity in my career and all that happy horseshit, and she ate it up. I came from an acting family, so I knew how to stay in role. I also knew I never wanted to cross her, for she could be quite vindictive. It still blows my mind that she was in charge of five states (AZ, NM, CO, UT, and Wyoming).

Under McKay were two ASACs, one of which was a good friend of mine from my Colorado days. His name was Joe Gordon. Joe had been Resident Agent in Charge (RAC) of the Colorado Springs Field Office, and he and I went back many years. He also was the Phoenix Field Division (PFD) foil to SAC McKay.

Though she never let it be known publicly (at least not verbally), she hated Gordon. I'm sure the feeling was mutual. Gordon had even tried a putsch against McKay utilizing Internal Affairs based on her inept leadership. The strategy backfired however and only because IA and Headquarters were afraid to go up against McKay; she was one of the highest ranking women in the agency. I think this factored into her leadership (or lack of) because she knew no one could touch her. As I said, she wasn't as stupid as some people thought.

The other ASAC was a man named Jason Lee*. Lee was a really good guy but not a person to get in the middle of McKay and Gordon's office wars. ASAC Lee just did his own thing and tried to keep the morale of the PFD office in good spirits. That didn't always work.

Over the first several weeks I realized that the morale in the division office was terrible. Most of the women hated each other, and when any one of them went to McKay with a beef, she just swept it under the rug. I witnessed many crying sessions in the office, and it killed me to see anyone endure any type of mind-fuck, especially from the condescending McKay. Yet, the PFD was "mind-fuck central."

My first assigned duties weren't very complicated or numerous. My principal job was overseeing the PFD motor pool. I was dubbed the "car guy." I was in charge of procuring vehicles, getting registrations/license plates, equipment installations, maintenance, etc., for every car in the five-state PFD fleet – something around 150 vehicles. At the time the PFD fleet was falling apart, so keeping all the vehicles running and on the road was a challenge, usually because of monetary issues – something I'll address later.

What SAC McKay didn't know or suspect was my true underlying duty in the PFD office – I was a mole for all the working agents in the field. ASAC Gordon had no problem with this because he actually cared about the working agents in the hinterlands; SAC McKay could have cared less. She only wanted to look good in the eyes of her superiors. Over the years I would keep everyone in the field apprised of what was happening in the division office.

As soon as I arrived in Phoenix McKay got her big chance to show off to the whole country, if not the world. The Winter Olympics were being held in Salt Lake City in 2002, and Utah was one of our states. McKay treated the Olympiad like it was a NASA moon landing, like it was the biggest thing to come around since V-E Day!

In actuality ATF's function in Salt Lake City was more of a support role to the FBI and Secret Service, but SAC McKay acted like she would be answering to chancellors and presidents from every country around the globe. Having been a political science major, I got a good chuckle out of this.

For all her posturing, ATF agents got stuck with shit details in Utah, like standing guard outside warehouses in the cold of night or inspecting every paper bag containing an exhausted forty-ounce bottle should it be a Molotov cocktail. I heard the detail was brutal, but McKay didn't care. To her this was her shot at history.

It was all a lie.

Here's another look inside McKay. When she arrived in Salt Lake City she went to pick up her rental car. All travel arrangements had been arranged by her secretary, and everything was supposedly in order; however, McKay went ballistic at the rental place because it had given her a white car when in reality she wanted a blue one (or vice versa). I'm not joking. I can't remember if she went to another rental company or not, but she eventually got the car she wanted, after burning up the phone and cussing out her secretary and everyone involved. We all got a huge laugh out of this in Phoenix, but that was McKay.

Many in the PFD office traveled to Salt Lake for the Olympics, but I luckily got to remain in Phoenix. I had just left a freezing state and had no intention of going back to one – especially to stand watch over some warehouse. Had I gone, however, I would have brought home many souvenirs.

McKay made sure that every allotted dollar was spent in outfitting all staff and agents with full winter gear (like each person was running in the Iditerod), Olympic memorabilia, and everything else that could be purchased. I would have loved to have seen the price tag on all that gear. She even made sure her friends in high places around the Bureau got detailed to SLC so they could join in all the booty. Again, it was all a farce. I had never seen such free-spending before, but this was only the tip of the iceberg on how ATF burned through cash.

Back in Phoenix I just decided to settle into my position as Senior Operations Officer (SOO). I had other duties besides being "car guy," but I basically just tried to help out around the PFD office. If any secretary or staff member needed help, I would assist. This got me in trouble with some people in the office. As stated, most of the women hated each other, so if I helped one with something I would be scorned by another. I didn't care because I'd help anyone, especially a staff member, but I was criticized by many for just being professional and nice. There's an old saying that if you lock two men in a room, after several hours they will emerge as friends. But, if you lock two women in a room and come back later, only one will walk out because she would have murdered the other. The PFD was the poster child of that adage. I tried not to let it bother me, and after some time I became friends with everyone.

Again, being a mole for the street agent was my primary concern. If anything bad was coming down the pike for a field agent or supervisor, I would tip him/her off. If it was warranted, I wouldn't say a thing, but 95 per cent of the time it was just cruel and undue punishment being dished out by the division office and McKay. She had her favorites and would play them accordingly. She would also play certain supervisors against other supervisors. She was a master puppeteer. After a while I learned who the "ins" were as well as the "outs." I also learned who the "rats" around the division were.

Now, I hate snitches with a passion, especially ATF agents who have nothing better to do. If your whole day revolves around you fucking someone else, then you got posted on my shit list. The PFD had several such people, and my biggest way of getting back at them took three steps: first, I would alert everyone around the PFD (or *nation* for that matter) who the snitch was; second, if that person ever asked anything of me, I would just throw the request in the trash; and third, if given a chance, I would make that person's life miserable. My reputation soon made its way around the field division, and after some time those on my shit list would avoid me altogether. Good. They should have been out arresting people, but they had other agendas.

Being in the PFD also gave me a chance to become privy to loads of information. McKay would hold staff meetings regularly, and during these conferences everything was discussed – from budget, to regulatory issues, to staffing, to furnishings – everything. Notice that none of these discussion points involved putting people in jail. If McKay didn't want you to hear something, then she would ask you to leave the room, which I gladly did when ordered. I hated staff meetings because usually nothing got said that meant anything. The people that spoke the most were usually the people who did the least, including Regional Counsel Joshua Rosen-Rosen, or R^2 from my Colorado days. R^2 always had the most to say which I thought was hilarious, because he couldn't find his tallywacker if his pants were on fire.

Another vociferous participant in these get-togethers was the head of Compliance/Regulatory, the ATF side of the house that dealt with the firearms and explosives industries. This guy also had a lot to talk about, but when I asked people in the office what he did exactly, no one seemed to have an answer. Like R^2, this guy made upwards of $120,000 per year. He and R^2 always spent time in each other's offices, so that told me right there. At least the compliance dude was a nice guy.

It wasn't long after arriving in Phoenix, and after the Olympics, that I got temporarily promoted to the position of Division Operations Officer, or DOO. Though temporary, this was a supervisory position. The DOO oversaw all the SOOs and basically made sure the PFD functioned smoothly from day to day. He/she also sat in on all conferences and was privy to everything going on in the division as well as nationally.

Talk about putting the fox in the henhouse! I soon became privy to all information, and during those nine months I became fairly schooled in all administrative operations of the Bureau. And, for the most part, what I saw disgusted me. Budget issues, especially.

The budget works as follows: Congress gives ATF so much money for the fiscal year, usually in the neighborhood of $800 million. After salaries are taken off the top (the biggest expense) the leftover amount is then broken up and distributed to headquarters directorates as well as the twenty-two or twenty-three field divisions around the country. Each field division was then autonomous in how it spent its money, though certain amounts fell within certain categories.

For example, there were investigative supplies, Agent Cashier Fund (monies to buy evidence), vehicle maintenance allowances, FEDEX allowances, travel allowances, everything down to allowances for having the morning paper delivered to the office. Each allowance was thereby assigned a code, and during the PFD budget meetings our Administrative Officer (the division employee who oversaw and monitored all expenditures) would basically tell the brass where we were in terms of how much was left in the kitty.

The first thing that floored me was how large the travel budget was. And, this money wasn't usually being spent by field agents. Most of the travel money was spent by the SAC and ASACs for travel all over the country and even internationally. Also, the inspectors from the regulatory side of the house burned through travel money, but this made sense because the PFD covered five states, and they did in fact have to journey to the hinterlands to conduct inspections of firearms and explosives dealers.

But as to why the SAC and ASACs traveled so much I had no idea.

Here's an example: the brass was in the habit of burning travel funds to attend retirement parties for other bosses around the country. Some *ad hoc* supervisors' conference would be scheduled justifying any and all travel to these going-away parties, and that pissed me off tremendously. I can't think of how many times I needed to travel for an investigation and was told I couldn't because there was no travel money available. Obviously, there was none available because the brass usually burned the bulk of it on frivolous journeys.

What I also learned in these budget meetings was that monies from one code could be moved to replenish another code. There were some limitations on this practice, but I soon came to see that if we were short on travel money, then money could be moved to build the travel fund right back up again. This usually left the other funds wanting – especially the Agent Cashier Fund which was primarily used to purchase evidence and pay informants. This fund was always dipped into, many times to the point where investigations had to be put on hold because of lack of funds to buy evidence. And I'm not talking about purchasing $20,000 worth of guns. There were times when an agent couldn't even buy a $20 rock of crack cocaine to secure a search warrant.

SAC McKay didn't give a shit, however. If an agent needed to develop probable cause to execute a search warrant, he/she would have to find another way; purchasing evidence was out. Besides, after reading the affidavit, McKay probably would shoot down the warrant anyway.

I also learned what the end of the fiscal year meant. If Congress gave us so much money for the fiscal year (October to September), then we had to spend every last penny; otherwise, the next fiscal budget would be less than the previous year. The end of the fiscal occurred every September, and those thirty days became a free-for-all of mostly frivolous expenditures. Vehicles in need of tires or windshields were usually taken care of, but many monies went to stuff like commemorative coins, shirts for employees, ATF mugs, signs, placards, and especially cash awards to agents.

All supervisors were told to put agents in for cash awards, even if they weren't truly deserving. In my career I had received a few cash awards which were nice, but I was making good money for the performance of my duties. Any excess money should have gone to the staff, who were living paycheck to paycheck, or to informants who were risking their lives. Some awards did in fact go to informants, but that was limited. The staff usually didn't get squat. Most if not all the cash went to agents around the division (or even other divisions).

By the time October 1 rolled around, all money was spent. The efficiency of the federal government and its agencies is suspect at best, but when it comes to spending money, it's a finely-greased precision machine.

Here's a good example of how to burn taxpayer money, and this occurred on several occasions, especially when McKay was in charge: call an All-Hand's Conference. These little get-togethers were scheduled usually after there had been some unexpected windfall of money added to the division budget. And, by windfall money, I mean taxpayer dollars or seized criminal assets that could have gone for better purposes. An All-Hand's Conference meant that everyone in the field division would travel to a specific city and meet for three or four days. An itinerary of topics would be discussed (to make the event seem kosher on paper in case we were ever audited), but for the most part it was one big party. ATF made Tailhook look like a backyard barbecue when it came to expenditure.

Over my entire career I attended two such outings: one in Los Angeles and one in Kansas City. However, in the Phoenix Field Division they occurred every couple of years. One was held in Vail; another in Rio Rico (Arizona); and, several in Phoenix proper. There was also a tri-division supervisors conference held in Las Vegas at the Hard Rock Café Hotel & Casino. Usually these meetings cost around $30 – $40,000, but I would have loved to see the final tab on that Vegas gig.

One All-Hand's Conference was pretty hilarious. It was held in Phoenix around 2003, and every agent and supervisor from five states descended upon the Valley of the Sun. It was cool to get to see my friends from Colorado Springs and Wyoming, and I made sure I showed everyone a good time.

For this particular conference I became "chauffeurman." I picked agents up at the airport and transported them back to the hotel. One such trip I picked up about seven Colorado Springs guys in my small government Chevy Malibu sedan. We were stuffed in like Vienna sausages.

That night, I took all these guys and several agents from Denver to a local bar by my apartment. Well, we just about trashed the place. The tavern had a beautiful granite bar, and as all the agents began doing shots of whisky and tequila, they began slamming the empty shot glasses on the bar. Bottles as well. I guess the surface of the bar sustained thousands of dollars of damage, but we didn't give a shit.

One agent from Denver got so shit-faced that I had to put him in my government car to sleep it off. An hour or two later I went out to check on him, only to find that he'd blown chunks all over the back seat of my car. He also had a wad of cash in his shirt pocket, about $200. I surreptitiously extricated the money and went back inside and paid the bar tab. To this day (or until he reads this) the agent thought he had lost the cash. I figured it was a fair exchange for throwing up in my car.

The All-Hand's Conference in Vail must have cost a fortune. Each day around 5 P.M., all the agents would go to the "Hospitality Suite." This was a separate hotel room which served only as a bar; the place was stocked with beer and booze from floor to ceiling. After the day's lectures, everyone (especially the brass) would head down to the hospitality suite to "get his/her drink on." We weren't called Alcohol, Tobacco and Firearms for nothing, for we could put away the booze. I'm not sure how all this stuff was paid for, but I know it didn't come out of my pocket.

I had a good time, but it was just another example of money being flushed down the toilet.

Here's another example of tons of taxpayer money being pissed away. There was a time when ATF had two successive Directors who had come over from the Secret Service (USSS). Most ATF personnel were upset that no one from within had been promoted, but indignation grew exponentially when we saw how these guys operated. Since they were appointed by the President, we were stuck with them.

The first USSS transplant created the Executive Protection Branch (EPB), and his successor kept it in operation. It remains so to this day. This branch was a new entity in ATF, and what it created was basically a large entourage what would accompany the Director on all his travels. And these guys traveled all the time.

It went like this. If the Director went on a multi-state trip (a common occurrence) to, say, Phoenix, Los Angeles, and Seattle, he would send an advance team or entourage to each destination days before to make any and all arrangements for the Director's protection within that particular city. Each city had a local agent point of contact (I was the POC for the Phoenix Field Division) and that agent had to basically coordinate the entire stay in his city. The POC and advance EPB agents (who were all SWAT members) would scout out locations, arrange for round-the-clock protection, and so forth.

Doing so put a heavy burden on local field divisions, but the Directors didn't care. They felt they were as important as the President and therefore had to be protected in the same way and at all costs. One of the Directors even insisted on being picked-up on the airport's tarmac precluding having to walk through the terminal. Some other agent or advance man would get the Director's bags at baggage claim (if he checked luggage). After procuring the bags we'd then give the Director a rented (with your taxpayer dollars) three-car Chevrolet Suburban escort to all pre-arranged locations. We couldn't use any PFD vehicles; the procession had to match a scene out of *Clear and Present Danger*.

Discretion and being incognito went out the window – which was a farce, because no citizen knew what these guys looked like; hell, I didn't even know what they looked like. Nonetheless, they wanted the royal treatment wherever they went. And of course they stayed at five-star hotels and ate at the finest restaurants. Up to that point ATF had always prided itself in being in the shadows, but these two and subsequent directors didn't give a shit. They wanted to be treated like the President. Such was the USSS mentality these two brought to ATF.

The point of this story is three-fold. First, the amount of money spent by the EPB had to be astronomical – taxpayer money of course. Second, this money could have gone to more worthy and needed causes, such as new cars for agents, money to buy evidence, promotions, new hires, etc. Third, it just illustrated how far ATF had come in getting away from its main mission – to put criminals behind bars. The Directors could have cared less about the latter; they just wanted to be treated like royalty. It seemed comical at the time, but in hindsight it was just another huge lie and egregious example of fraud, waste and abuse.

As interim DOO I also got to sit in on numerous panels for prospective new hires. As I would soon learn, the hiring process in ATF was a far cry from what it had been when I was hired. As a result of many lawsuits filed against ATF regarding the hiring process and promotions – mostly brought by minorities – the new hiring procedure was more regimented. Each prospective agent was asked the same questions, the same scenarios, the same *everything*.

When I got hired in 1990 it was a crap shoot. I remember the day I had my interview with SAC Andrew Vita and his ASAC, who happened to be from New York and very sharp. I fielded scenario questions from all over the place. There was no way I could have studied or even been prepared for it.

I remember one scenario the ASAC put to me. He asked the following: "Let's say you are in a car following another car which contains an undercover agent and a bad guy. Suddenly, you cross a bridge over a creek and you see a little baby drowning in the water. What would you do?" I thought about this for a minute and replied, "Well, my first duty is to protect and serve the public. Since my partner in the undercover car is trained in being in role and should be able to handle himself (he had so far), then I would have pulled over to the side and saved the baby from drowning." The ASAC smirked at me and then retorted, "Well, what if the baby had only been a doll?" I could only look down into my lap and then up again to rejoin the ASAC's eyes. "Well," I said, "then I guess the joke was on me." He nodded, and the interview continued.

Many months later and after I'd been hired, that same ASAC would tell me that I had given the correct answer; he also said that he had pulled that scenario out of his ass. That was the old way of conducting a panel interview: you had to think on your feet.

The new scenarios presented to the applicants were more tightly scripted and generic. All that which was esoteric, or out of left field, was out the window. We as panel interviewers couldn't even ask any extemporaneous questions of the applicant. It was *that* tightly scripted.

There were two sets of scenario questions (maybe 18 in all), and each prospective applicant would be presented with eight or nine scenarios. There were three possible answers to each question. The best answer would receive a score of "4," the second best answer, a "3," and the last answer a "2," or non-passing score. No scores were divulged to the applicant, but if any "2" was scored, then the applicant was automatically not-hired.

Most of the scenarios dealt with ethics issues. Example: "Suppose you're on a search warrant and you see your partner pocket some money from a drawer, what would you do?" There were a lot of questions like this, with the best answer always being you'd go run and tell the supervisor on scene. A "3" answer in this case would be you would tell the thief agent that you saw him take the money and to put the shit back. The "2" answer would be you wouldn't say anything.

Now, over my career I witnessed agents taking stuff – usually money – and I never said a goddamn thing, for I looked deeper into the situation. More often than not the agent taking the cash had many mouths at home to feed and the federal salary just wasn't cutting it (we weren't allowed to work other jobs at the time). Who was I to judge another agent's actions? Besides, it was just dope money anyway. In other words, I probably would have flunked the new scenario test.

As stated, the underlying theme of most of the scenarios was to rat out your partner or another agent. It was also easy to see that many applicants had been coached before the panel interview, especially prospective agents who had fathers in high places or buddies or relatives already in the Bureau. I've never been a fan of nepotism in any aspect, but this took it to a new level.

I looked at the hiring process this way: the person sitting across from me right now may be called upon someday to save my life or someone else's; would he/she be able to do that? I know he/she will rat me out to my boss, but will he/she be able to step up to the plate at the eleventh hour with the shit hitting the fan? That's what I looked for in each applicant, but it really had no place in the interviewing process.

I remember interviewing one kid whose father was a United States Attorney (appointed by the President) from some judicial district in the Rocky Mountains. His application file went straight to the top of the stack, and this kid whizzed through the scenario section of the interview. He was answering questions before they were even put to him. It was a joke. He passed with flying colors. I don't know if we ever hired him, but I do know one thing, I wouldn't have wanted him going through a door with me. I could just see it in his eyes and his deportment.

Basically the hiring process had become (and still is) a joke. We were only looking for robots. I think of the dozens of applicant interviews I sat in on, maybe one or two were deemed undesirable. And, of the 90 per cent who were hirable, most were folks you wouldn't want in a foxhole with you. In regards to the one or two who were undesirable, we on the panel had to write extensive reasons as to why we thought the applicant should not be hired. We had to write more about the undesirables than about the good prospects, only because ATF was afraid of getting sued at a later date by the rejected applicant. And, if the applicant was a minority, then holy shit! We would have to write a thesis on why this person was denied.

After these days were over I felt sick to my stomach – not because of the process, but rather because I had had a hand in putting these less-than-ideal agents on the street to support my fellow agents who had *earned* the right to be investigators. There was nothing I could do; the hiring process was now so structured and regimented that a monkey could have been hired if coached accordingly.

It was several months after the Olympics that SAC McKay got her ultimate wish; she was promoted and brought into headquarters as a Deputy Assistant Director (whatever that position entailed, which was usually nothing). It was good news for her, but even greater news for everyone in the PFD. I equate it to Dorothy's house falling on the Wicked Witch of the East.

McKay's replacement was a guy named Buster Parkes*, and he was a great guy. The only problem with Parkes was he was a short-timer, that is, he wasn't going to be around for long because he was close to retirement.

I didn't know a lot about Parkes, and in ATF circles that's usually a good thing. I did know that he cared about putting people in jail, something McKay could have cared less about. Her main task was to create focus groups, have get-togethers, and spend money.

Parkes subsequently met with each person in the division office in a face-to-face meeting. I'd never seen a SAC do this, let alone *any* boss. I was impressed. When my turn came to meet him, I went into his office and sat down nervously. I was always nervous sitting in a SAC's office, but Buster kept me at ease.

After some small talk he asked me point-blank, "What is my biggest challenge in the Phoenix Field Division?" He had come from Kentucky or Charlotte – I can't remember – so he really was looking for insight in tackling his newly-received five-state field division. He was very sincere, and I liked him from that very moment because I knew he would listen to what I had to say. I looked him in the eye and replied, "Denver. Denver is your biggest challenge. Getting the agents to hit the streets hard will be your biggest challenge, because for the most part, all they want to do is go home for the evening. Denver is virgin territory and rife with crime." I was adamant, and I knew Buster took in every word.

It was soon thereafter that the Denver offices were raped, pillaged, and plundered by Buster and ASAC Gordon. Denver agents were finally forced to do their jobs. Forced?! You would think they would have wanted to perform their duties. Denver agents were responding to every gun call at all hours of the day and night. Many complained, but their gripes fell on deaf ears. I would receive calls (again, I was the mole, though I loved what was being done in Denver) from Denver agents saying, "They [the brass] have us working like police officers. We're trained and expert investigators. We work complex cases and put people away for many years." "Well," I said, "That's great. Now, get back to doing just that."

Problem was, no one in Denver was doing shit – with few exceptions – and SAC Parkes and ASAC Gordon knew it. I was playing both sides of the fence, but someone needed to kick Denver in the ass, and thanks to Parkes and Gordon, it got done. Ben Maxwell, who had recently been promoted to supervisor, was thankful as well. For too long Denver had been the vacation spot of ATF. Well, not anymore.

Sorry, folks – but I did have a hand in that.

SAC Parkes also took me under his wing, and his first order of business was to get me back on the street and out of the administrative office. If I haven't said it, a monkey could have done my job in administration. I was usually done by lunchtime with the day's daily duties; so, the rest of the day was spent finding things to do. I even began studying in the afternoon to stay busy. Chemistry, physics, geometry, French: I taught myself all kinds of shit. I would even go downstairs and take a nap in an empty office at times. Again, taxpayer dollars at work.

Looking for things to do, I quickly became the troubleshooter of the PFD. Buster knew this and appreciated my dedication, but he still wanted to see me back in an enforcement group. Knowing my troubled history with the United States Attorney's Offices (USAO), his first order of business was to arrange meetings with the Phoenix USAO to discuss my past and more importantly my future. I did not sit in on any of these meetings, but the USAO made it clear to Buster that it thought my past would preclude me from working independently. However, the USAO saw no problem with me working in conjunction with other agents.

For example, I could not be a sole affiant on a search warrant; yet, I could be co-affiant with another agent. Also, I could be a finder of evidence as long as another agent was present as a corroborating witness. Minus the embarrassment, after time my reliability and integrity would augment. I told Buster that that arrangement was fine with me, though I was somewhat perplexed that I could testify in one judicial district but not another.

Example. While in Phoenix I was subpoenaed by the Judicial District of New Jersey to testify in a federal case there. The suspect was a guy named Carl Sanks* who I had been working in Denver and who had trafficked over 80 firearms to the Newark (NJ) area. The case was interesting in that the suspect had no criminal record (thus the reason he could buy guns, and *of course*, he was making all the purchases from Georgia Pawn).

However, this guy was dirty; anyone buying in excess of eighty low-end handguns usually was. Also, he had a cousin who worked at Denver International Airport (DIA). This cousin had full and unlimited access to DIA and security was lax (this was pre-9/11). It was believed that he was simply putting the firearms on planes to be flown to New Jersey. All it took was someone on the other end to unload the contraband and distribute. By the time the planes hit the tarmac at Newark International, all the trafficked firearms had obliterated serial numbers. Yet, after some time and after many guns had turned up in crime scenes, several serial numbers were forensically raised by the police laboratories. This led straight back to Sanks.

Sanks was subsequently arrested and tried in New Jersey. I flew back to testify, and when I met the Assistant United States Attorneys (AUSAs) on the case, I told them of my history. They researched it fully and told me nothing in my past precluded me from testifying in the Sanks' case. Sanks was ultimately convicted and sent to federal prison.

The Arizona AUSAs, however, weren't as understanding. Nevertheless, and because of SAC Parkes' savoir faire and leadership skills, the Phoenix USAO agreed to let me go back on the street, provided I adhered to their parameters.

Around 2005, I was transferred to Phoenix Group V, the Arson & Explosives Group. It wasn't my first choice, but I was in no position to bargain. I took the assignment with pride and bid goodbye to all the friends I had made in the division office. I wouldn't be moving too far away however – only downstairs. Everyone was happy for my transfer, though none of the staff wanted me to leave. I made a habit of going upstairs to visit because the women in the division office were great people. Under Buster, they were finally getting the recognition they deserved.

And me, I was off to the bomb group.

Chapter XXV

Chili Cook-Off

The following is good example of how *not* to cover an undercover operation. If you don't already know, covering a deal involves many agents giving support to a fellow agent who is meeting with criminals in an undercover capacity. Depending on the situation, the number of cover agents can number anywhere from six or seven to several dozen. The undertaking described below had a minimal amount of cover agents due to the fact there was to be no exchange of goods or contraband; it was only to involve conversation in the hopes of setting up a transaction at a later date. Little did any of us know, this undertaking wouldn't involve as much cover as it would involve "under the covers."

It all started one afternoon when two men walked into the ATF office wishing to speak with an agent. This was an uncommon occurrence, and since my partner and I happened to be available, we sat down with the two citizens to see what they had to say. The main guy owned his own security company, and his friend was basically second-in-charge. Their story was interesting and also up our alley.

Apparently one of the security guards in the company was trying to sell handguns to fellow employees. This individual's past, according to his boss, was shady, but subsequent investigation showed that he (the suspect) didn't have any felony convictions or serious arrests. Any case against him would have to be dealing without a federal firearms license, a difficult investigation in that we would have to make a series of buys to show that he was engaged in the business of selling firearms and was making a profit. The latter two points were the most important elements of the crime.

Proving those elements may sound simple, but the United States Attorney's Office (USAO) was reluctant to prosecute those types of cases – especially against someone who had a minor criminal record at best. They also cost a lot of money, but for the most part we didn't care.

I in turn reached out to an Assistant US Attorney and asked if the USAO would be interested in prosecuting such a case; I presented all the facts and told the AUSA that all elements of the offense would be perfected before the case was submitted. The AUSA expressed his interest, and we decided to pursue the investigation.

The strategy we would use was the following: my partner, in an undercover role, would join the security company as another employee and attempt to get close to the gun seller and eventually make a series of firearm purchases. Sounded good on paper, but as was usually the case, the investigation would take on a life of its own.

The first undercover operation was arranged one evening at a local nightclub. The security company provided protection for the venue, and it seemed like a good place to start. My partner was rigged with a radio transmitter/wire and began his "career" as a bouncer at the aforementioned club. I also had another agent working undercover stationed in the nightclub as cover should anything go awry. I gave each undercover agent an amount of Agent Cashier Fund (ACF) should they wish to purchase any drinks inside. This became a learning lesson, since both agents left the place later that night with a hefty bar tab which I would later have to explain to my boss. Lesson learned: don't ever give cover agents $100 of ACF to quench their thirst. Just flip them twenty dollars out of your own wallet and live with the "investment."

I sat in a car with another agent outside the club to record any and all conversation between the undercover agent and the suspect. Since the nightclub was having a Battle of the Bands that evening, any recording of what went on inside sounded like putting a microphone inside a jet engine; it was worthless. I should have known better, but we were required to always wire up the undercover agent.

After the show the undercover agent told me that he had made some small talk with the suspect but nothing really in regards to firearms. He basically just got to know the suspect. That was only my intention, and we prepared for the next meeting.

The next event the security company supported was a chili cook-off at large hotel resort. This seemed like a better venue in that any and all communications wouldn't have to compete with Van Halen covers or guitar feedback. The operation was set and basically would be like the last: one agent working undercover as a security guard while another agent and I would act like ordinary citizens attending the event.

Unfortunately this arrangement didn't go as planned.

Since the cook-off was being held at a hotel, I rented a room that would serve as the base for the operation. It was a standard room with two queen-size beds and would be a good place for all of the agents to crash later. It would also be a good spot to monitor and record all conversation.

The security guards, undercover included, had to arrive early to the event to make sure everything was in place. The owner of the company was supposed to be there as well to supervise, but for some reason he was running late. When the event opened, the undercover went in role and did what he had to do; also, the cover agent paid admission and would just mill around the contest. I decided to wait for the security owner in the hotel room until he arrived. I would also set up all the recording equipment.

What the owner arrived with was hardly what I expected.

About an hour into the event, the owner shows up with two women, one under each arm – and *hot* women! I played it off, but as I got to talking with the owner, it became clear that he'd brought the two girls for a reason. And it wasn't to be judges at the chili-fest.

It couldn't have been thirty minutes before both of us had paired off with the two females and were going to town. I'd had a few one-night stands in my time, but I don't think I'd ever made it into the sack that quickly. I didn't know what to think, but being a man I just let events progress where they may.

During all this time I kept getting calls from the two undercover agents, but I let the calls go unanswered. I was too engaged in what I was doing. Besides, the recording equipment was working perfectly. However, there could have been a shoot-out at the event, but I didn't care. Besides, I knew the two undercovers would know what to do should any trouble arise – chance of which seemed unlikely.

A few hours later (yes, it went that long) I heard a banging on the hotel room door. My acting boss that day was supposedly coming down to the event, so I didn't know who was knocking. Hopefully it wasn't him. The two girls quickly arose and dashed into the bathroom. The security owner and I quickly got out of bed, wrapped towels around our waists and happily gave each other "high fives" for what had just transpired. I made my way to the door to answer.

What I didn't find out until later was that the two agents standing outside the room, the undercover and the cover agent, had been looking through the window. All they saw were two guys in towels giving each other high fives in the middle of the room. The agents didn't know what to think, but I can imagine.

I subsequently opened the door and went outside to talk to them. To this day I can't put into words the look these guys had on their faces. It was priceless! I shut the door behind me and asked nonchalantly how the event was going and all that happy horseshit and told the agents I'd be down shortly. They only shook their heads in laughter and went back to the event. I in turn quickly got dressed and went back to work.

You talk about an interesting dinner break.

We never did purchase any firearms from the suspect, despite all the Agent Cashier Funds spent on the investigation. I had to answer for this at a later date, but my boss was cool with me. Sometimes cases just fizzled out into the "no potential" realm.

At least I made several new friends – one especially.

Chapter XXVI

Arson & Explosives

Going to the A & E group was a great opportunity for me for several reasons. First, I knew very little about bombs, pyrotechnics, and fire investigations, even though I was a huge chemistry buff; second, the people in the group were all seasoned veterans, many of whom I had known for many years. The group supervisor (GS) was a woman named Stacy Wright*, and she was a great and knowledgeable boss. I had known her for years while she was stationed in the San Francisco area as well as from the Academy. After working for Georgia McKay, I was a little leery about working for another female, but Stacy was everything you could want in a supervisor – male *or* female. She also knew her shit when it came to arson and explosives.

My co-workers, as stated, were also seasoned vets. Arthur Knight*, who had cast a huge shadow at Columbine (see Chapter XIX), was the leader of the group, but he was surrounded by other very knowledgeable agents. They all took me in like family, and I am forever grateful. GS Wright was the same way.

Being a glutton for knowledge, I knew I'd be learning a lot in Group V. I had received some explosives training at the Academy, but that had been nearly fifteen years before. Moreover, I had learned over the years that if I stumbled upon a bomb or improvised explosive device (IED), I would get the hell out of there and call in the experts. Well, now *I* was to become one of the experts – to some extent anyway – and I looked forward to it with great anticipation.

GS Wright initially sent me to a post-blast school in Orlando. This was a great refresher course in everything from bomb recognition, IED reassembly, and overall explosive investigation. I mopped up the curricula like crazy. Besides, it was interesting stuff.

I also attended a Chemistry of Pyrotechnics (i.e., fireworks) School at Washington College in Chestertown (MD). The curricula were somewhat dry, but for me it was like being back in high school chemistry class (but without having the windows shot out by gangbangers). I ate it up. I had studied some chemistry in college – more in the area of nuclear physics as it pertained to foreign policy; those were the Reagan/Cold War years, but this class was awesome. I learned so much, and afterward spoke to the instructor on a regular basis if I had any questions in the field – which were many.

I also learned and assisted in giving explosives demonstrations in Arizona. We would go to some landfill in Glendale (AZ), and put on huge explosive shows for state and local law enforcement officers. Sometimes even the press would be invited. The displays were awesome. I was just happy that I got to help out.

I also learned how to shoot fireworks professionally. And, I'm not talking about laying on the ground and shooting a bottle-rocket out of your ass, a la *Jackass*. I'm talking about the huge pyrotechnic shows that take place on the Fourth of July and at the Super Bowl. Phoenix was home to one of the biggest pyrotechnics companies in the world, and each year I would attend a symposium where I would learn how to shoot fireworks in such big displays. It was awesome! Moreover, the pyrotechnics folks were always great to us, and I learned tons of stuff from them.

It's not as easy as it looks; in fact, it is quite a dangerous undertaking – so, my hat's off to those men and women who do it for a living, all for our enjoyment. I was scared at first, but after learning the ropes, I became semi-confident that I could run a pyrotechnics show at a football game or a Metallica concert (and I promise James, you'd be safe this time).

The greatest thing about being in Group V was the camaraderie. Everyone worked each other's cases, and that was good because I didn't know anything at first. It was the best group I had been in since my Los Angeles days, and it's no fluke that several of the agents in Group V had come from the LA Field Division. We may have not been putting people in jail on a nightly basis like some of the gun groups, but in terms of knowledge and experience, no field office could touch us. And, that was a good feeling.

I remember one of the first incidents we were called out on. Apparently an employee of the Palo Verde Nuclear Power Plant – which sits approximately 50 miles due west of Phoenix – had tried to drive through security with an IED (pipe bomb) in the bed of his pickup truck. Now, this was post-9/11, and being that Palo Verde is the biggest nuclear power plant in the country, this was no laughing matter. It became a scene right out of *The China Syndrome*.

I drove out there in my government car at warp speed. When I got to the site, there were cops and emergency crews everywhere. It reminded me of Columbine to an extent. There were also choppers circling in the sky, and I was told that the entire plant was in lockdown mode until all the facts could be sifted through.

It turns out that the employee with the pickup truck – who undoubtedly felt like shit because he had disrupted power generation to millions of people in several states that day – had tried to drive into the complex with the aforementioned IED in the back of his truck, and all unbeknownst to him. Apparently, some kids or another sick individual had just tossed the thing in the back as a gag. He's lucky the thing didn't detonate.

I owned a truck at the time and I never looked in the back to see what might or might not be there. Soda cans usually. After that day, however, I *always* checked.

The Department of Energy (who runs the US nuclear plants) treated the guy like he was al-Qaeda. Once the facts started surfacing, I really felt bad for him. We ended up searching his apartment, doing follow-up interviews, everything. Hopefully he didn't lose his job, but I bet he did. Knowing the federal government, they probably blamed him for locking down Palo Verde for six to eight hours. It was pretty hilarious after all the dust had settled. Better safe than sorry, I guess.

Another thing I learned in Phoenix was that people in Arizona liked their explosives. We were getting called out constantly. In my whole career I had probably been called out on five bombings or explosives incidents. In Phoenix it was every week! The saying around the office was "tweakers like their bombs." Translation: methamphetamine users like to screw around with things that go boom! We also had two full-time Explosive Enforcement Officers (EEOs) stationed in Scottsdale, and these guys were always busy. These folks had all the equipment to render explosives safe. This usually meant blowing the things in place. They were great guys, too.

For some reason, the bomb guys in ATF were the coolest dudes. I can't put my finger on it, but it must have been because ice ran through their veins. These guys were perfectionists, but they had to be. One wrong move and you were stuck to the ceiling. Even at the Academy, the explosives instructors were always the best people. Probably because there was no story you could tell that they couldn't top. I respected the shit out of these men and women. I still do.

My first case in the Arson & Explosives Group was a big one. It involved the burning down of a commercial strip mall in Gilbert (AZ). One night around 2 A.M. (for some reason *all* suspicious fires occurred at these hours), the whole place just went up in smoke. Since the blaze did such extensive damage, the ATF National Response Team (NRT) was called in.

The NRT were a crack unit that would come in and assist any local fire or police department in a bombing investigation or suspected arson should it be requested. The members of the NRT were seasoned veterans and had seen things exponentially worse than I'd ever seen. My respect for these men and women is incalculable.

The NRT arrived the next day and hit the ground running. Since they'd worked so many similar scenes, they had a game-plan from the get-go. Interviews were set up, digging out the scene was coordinated; everything was logistically mastered by the NRT. I had seen them in the field before, but not at ground zero, as they say. This was my case and I was the case agent, so I was in awe of what I saw going on around me.

I soon realized that I was proud to be an ATF agent again. That was a feeling I hadn't felt in a long time, especially in my days behind the desk. I was proud to wear my fire hat and fire boots (thank you Stacy). I didn't know what I was doing, but I was proud to be there that day. The NRT team wrapped up its investigation in a day or two and all reports were handed to me like I had ordered them from room service. It was that tight of a unit.

The final determination was that some oily rags had spontaneously combusted, and sent the strip mall falling to the ground in the middle of the night in a huge conflagration. So, the only real mess was with the insurance companies, but that wasn't my balliwick. But again, I had learned so much in so short a time span. It felt great. And it was made possible by SAC Parkes and GS Knight.

I was an ATF agent again.

Being in the A & E Group also had its fringe benefits, that is, especially if you liked sports, notably football. Tempe and Glendale hosted annual college football bowl games, and the National Football League held Super Bowl XLII in Glendale in 2008. GS Wright was always smart enough to plan for these events in advance, and she was a guru at getting the ATF brass to fund the event from the law enforcement side.

Huge football games are believed to be major targets of terrorists, so ATF (actually, GS Wright) took the reins and made sure the venue was completely safe for the subsequent game. The jury is out on whether or not this tax payer money was well-spent, but I do know I got to watch some pretty good football games. Nothing bad ever happened, so my hat's off to GS Wright and all the ATF people that came in, especially the ATF canine crews. Everyone was totally professional and serious in the performance of their duties. However, we (ATF) used the whole extravaganza to toot our own horn. Thanks to the asshole who bombed the Summer Olympics in Atlanta in 1996, every sport venue is now gone over with a fine-toothed comb. And at a very large expense, I might add.

A time came in 2007 or 2008 where the Phoenix Division office was to be inspected. These administrative inspections occurred every two or three years and for the most part they were a joke. People from Internal Affairs would come in and go over all the administrative files, car files, speak with local law enforcement chiefs and prosecutors – just to get a feel for how well the Phoenix Field Division was functioning.

When SAC McKay was around, these inspections became meticulous to say the least. It reminded me of the drill instructor in *Full Metal Jacket* inspecting the bunks of all the grunts in his platoon. It was all a big charade. As long as all the money and property were in order, everything else was window dressing.

The auditors, as we called them, would do their week-long inspection and then would prepare a formal report of its findings which would be presented to the SAC at a later date. Once we received the report from IA, it was my job to prepare a formal memorandum to the auditors specifically documenting how we were to correct any problems in the future.

These memos were nearly twenty pages long! If the auditors said that a car file was unacceptable because the agent had not logged his last oil change, then I would have to include in my memo that "all agents in the future will be told or retold to enter such crucial data in the file." I'm not making this up; this is how petty it got.

Property was another story. I was also the "Property Guy" while in the division office. What that meant was I was accountable, and hence the SAC was accountable, for every piece of property in the field division. Five states! Most items had a PIN (personal identifier number), but during the division office reviews, finding some of this shit wasn't easy. We had radios on telephone poles in Wyoming. We had undercover cars equipped with hidden audio/visual equipment. We also had radio repeaters on top of Pike's Peak in Colorado.

Someone had to go look and inspect all this gear for the inspection. It was harrowing! Most of the auditors didn't give a shit, because they weren't agents or law enforcement people. But, the "bean counters" made everyone's lives miserable trying to find certain items. Miraculously, we passed all the property audits, though I did have to write a ton of memos stating that certain items could not be found.

The division office audit/inspections only occurred every two years, but it was a hectic time nonetheless. I became amazed that ATF could get *anything* done with all the microscopic oversight from above. Thank God I never got into management. But the big question was what these inspections cost, for not only did an inspection team come to Phoenix, but also to every field office in the division. Moreover, we were only one field division out of 22 or 23, and these Internal Affairs teams were responsible for inspecting every field division every couple years. The cost had to be astronomical.

In 2007 the Phoenix Field Division was due for another inspection, and since I had been through two such shakedowns, I volunteered to help out the division office. I wasn't doing much in the Arson & Explosives Group, so I offered my services to the new SAC who was a good guy. It was supposed to be a temporary thing, but I knew I'd never get back to Group V. That was okay, because I had learned so much while being in that group. But, I knew I wasn't a bomb guy. I was a gang guy, and if I couldn't arrest gang members off the street, then my best contribution to the Bureau was back in administration looking out for the agents on the street.

So, I went back upstairs, and that would be my ultimate downfall.

Chapter XXVII

Cheese Heads

Wisconsin is known for many things: dairy products, hunting, and the Green Bay Packers. It also is known for an assorted array of infamous characters: Jeffrey Dahmer (who liked to keep human remains in his icebox); Ed Gein (of dead skin mask fame and *Psycho*); and staunch survivalists. I had never been to the Cheese State, but that would change one winter afternoon after a certain individual was arrested in north Phoenix.

At the time I was assigned to the Arson & Explosives Group, Phoenix Group V, and on a certain day we assisted in a search warrant in north Phoenix. The suspect was a reclusive kind of guy but who had many interesting hobbies: he liked to make explosives, keep exotic animals (preferably, gila monsters), possess a multitude of firearms, and he also had a keen interest in the manufacture of ricin, a toxic agent easily extracted from castor beans.

Post 9/11, much attention has been given to illicit ricin production, but its history goes back much further. Several governments looked into its feasibility as a chemical/biological warfare agent during WWI and WWII. When ingested the ricin wreaks havoc on the body and can lead to death. It is believed that al-Qaeda has experimented with its use as well.

During the warrant execution or maybe before, it was learned that the suspect was from upstate Wisconsin. Federal and local officials soon descended upon the suspect's residence in Wisconsin to conduct a follow-up warrant. What they found was something out of a Hollywood movie. The guy had built a two-story shed, bigger than most dual-level homes, but it had no electricity, running water or other amenities. It appeared that any strong gust of wind would blow the place down, but somehow it had managed to remain on its foundation. Evidence recovered at the site was vast: many rifles, tons of ammunition, and lots of survivalist type wares: handbooks, canned foods, animal traps, snow equipment, etc. The Feds gathered up only the weapons and ammunition, and it was later agreed that the suspect would be tried in Arizona on a multitude of charges, notably the ricin.

The ATF agent assigned to the case was Arthur Knight*, a seasoned agent who I had known from my Los Angeles days. He had also cast an interesting shadow during the Columbine case (see Chapter XIX). Knight was one of most knowledgeable agents I ever met, though he did have a flair for the dramatic. Every investigation of his, according to him, usually had tentacles extending across the entire globe – if not into outer space – but his work was commendable. He was a great guy, and I learned a lot from him, especially in the areas of arson and explosives. So, Knight dove into the case hard.

While the suspect was locked up in a local Phoenix jail, Knight soon learned that he was making numerous phone calls to a wife or girlfriend back in Wisconsin. These conversations, unbeknownst to the crook (unbelievably!), were monitored and recorded – tapes of which were procured by Knight. Many of us in Group V began listening to the tapes and soon realized that the suspect kept asking his wife about the warrant execution back in Wisconsin, especially about whether or not the feds had looked in the walls.

It soon became apparent that the warrant hadn't uncovered everything, and that odds were good that the suspect had stashed some items, probably firearms, behind the drywall. Knight soon procured another federal warrant for the "house" in Wisconsin, and he and I flew back there to direct the search. We would soon meet up with some local ATF agents out of the Milwaukee office who would aid in the warrant execution.

The trip back to Wisconsin is worth mentioning because it was the trip from hell. When booking travel, all ATF agents were required to use a particular federal travel agency (undoubtedly another example of federal government nepotism). The agency would usually find the most direct flights and book all reservations, including cars and hotels. Since Knight and I didn't know Wisconsin from Siberia, we just received our itineraries online from the travel agency and subsequently drove to the airport. That proved to be a huge mistake.

Since the warrant site was in the northern part of Wisconsin, we had to fly to several airports to get there. First we had to fly to Minneapolis, jump a connector to Milwaukee, and then a third puddle-jumper to an airport in the hinterlands – Rhinelander I believe. Had we done any research on our own and had a foreshadowing of what was to come, we would have just flown straight to Minneapolis, rented a car, and driven three hours to our destination. Little did we know that would have saved us six or seven hours of travel.

Once we got to Milwaukee we boarded a two-engine prop job to take us to Rhinelander. I have a small fear of flying, especially on a twenty-seat midget plane, but I sucked it up because I had no alternative. We were delayed somewhat in Milwaukee, but soon took off to the Great White North. The ride was pretty smooth but I had white knuckles notwithstanding. Forty-five minutes into the flight, the captain (who couldn't have been older than 25) turned to the passengers (yes, he was that close) and informed us that we'd be returning to Milwaukee because the altimeter on the plane was not functioning. More white knuckles.

The captain said we had to return to Milwaukee to have the altimeter fixed or replaced. What about another plane? I asked. None was available. Great! Seemed harmless enough, but I kept asking myself how this guy was going to land a plane without any altitude gauge. Well, he pulled it off, and thus we were all set back another hour or two before the plane could be repaired.

Eventually we took off and made it to Rhinelander sometime after midnight. We then had to drive an additional hour or two north to get to our ultimate destination. I remember in Rhinelander that all the rental car places were closed – adding to our frustration even more – but somehow we were able to secure a vehicle. We arrived at the "hotel," which was actually a hunting cabin next to a lake, sometime around 2 A.M. After four or five hours of sleep we were on the road again, this time to the warrant site. Suffice it to say, that was the last time I ever booked an official flight through that travel agency. They suck!

We met the Milwaukee agents at a café early the next morning and drove out to serve the warrant. It was extremely cold that morning and had begun to snow. On arriving at the site, we were met by some FBI agents and some local police who were there to assist.

As stated, the residence was fairly large – at least 2000 square feet, so we weren't exactly sure where to begin. We even had x-ray machines to use on the walls, though for whatever reason, these didn't function properly. We also had to bring in gas generators and lighting equipment so we could see what we were doing, for it was pitch-black inside. As I first ventured inside I nearly broke my leg. . . several times. There were holes in the floor, some visible, some not. I decided to back out until we got sufficient lighting, which soon arrived. Knight decided that we would go room to room; we would carefully remove all drywall and see if anything was hidden behind.

What we found I'll never forget. Behind every wall in the residence – first and second story – was gear assembled by a survivalist who was obviously preparing for Armageddon; he had everything. I thought I had walked into a Cabela's or Bass Pro Shop. He had generators, motorcycles, bicycles, bear traps, snow shoes, skis, ammo, food, gas lamps, propane, winter clothing, and over 100 rifles. Each long gun was individually wrapped in weather-resistant plastic and water-resistant cloth. He even had stuff buried in the yard in huge PVC pipes. He had enough weaponry to start a war of his own. He also had gold coins wrapped up in cloth and plastic, and other monies or items that could be bartered with whoever should survive the end of time.

In my nearly 20 years on the job I had never seen anything like it. I had found guns and dope behind walls before, but nothing like this makeshift sporting goods store. I guess I was even impressed to some extent. Again, another valuable lesson learned during a search.

The next big task was how to get all the evidence out and to a safe location. We had to order a semi-tractor trailer to haul the stuff away which didn't get there for several hours. I don't think we got out of there until deep into the night, and as the day had progressed, the snow had continued to fall. Nonetheless, it was a great hit, and I was happy Knight had brought me along. We would leave sometime the next day, and yes, on the same route we had come.

What I remember most about that day was talking with a local Sheriff's deputy. I asked him if he had ever seen such a place, because I sure as shit hadn't. He could only look at me and laugh, and what he told me I'll never forget. He said that if we conducted warrants on about 75 per cent of the local residents of these parts, we'd probably find the same thing. I asked him if he was using hyperbole; he only brushed off the snow and replied, "I *wish* I was joking."

The suspect eventually would go to federal prison for the ricin and several other charges. It was the first time anyone had gone to prison in Arizona for ricin manufacture, and it was a huge feather in Knight's hat. Well-deserved, I must say.

Chapter XXVIII

Katrina

In late August 2005, the Gulf Coast area of the United States, and especially New Orleans, were just about destroyed by Hurricane Katrina. It became the costliest natural disaster in US history – three times as costly as Hurricane Andrew in 1992. Several weeks later, Hurricane Rita forged her own disastrous path, leaving western Louisiana and southeastern Texas in shambles. Hundreds of thousands of people became displaced, and thanks to cable news, these tragedies were plastered across every television set around the world. What happened in the aftermath (or what *didn't* happen) is well-documented, and I won't get into that controversial subject in these pages. However, when asked later what I would compare all the destruction to, I could only conjure up Hiroshima. Many would take me to task for this comparison; I'm just saying it was the first thing that came to mind. The tsunami that hit Japan in March 2011 is a more likely and current analogy, but this was 2005.

I had recently been transferred to the Phoenix Arson & Explosives Group, and I soon got word that each ATF field division would have to deploy several agents to go to Louisiana in the latter part of September 2005. Since I was new to the group and had no open investigations, I knew I'd be chosen, but I preempted that selection process because I wanted to go. Not for any fame or fortune – hell, I had no idea what I was getting into – I just knew people were in need of help, and that was what I was paid to do.

When the departure date arrived, my partner Darian* and I loaded up two SUVs and began driving in tandem towards the Deep South. I knew Interstate-10 was the principal escape route out of Louisiana (and everywhere for that matter), so Darian and I decided to take I-40 east (a route I was familiar with) to Little Rock, Arkansas, and then head south into Louisiana. This proved to be a good maneuver because I-10 was a mess in so many ways. And miraculously, we only got pulled over by a highway patrolman once because we were flying!

On arriving in New Orleans I couldn't believe what I saw. The waters had receded upon arrival, but the devastation was harrowing. You could see the waterlines on the houses, many of which were 15-20 feet up the exterior walls. All furnishings, personal belongings, and knickknacks had been washed out of the homes and littered the streets. The stench was appalling. I remember the rats: they were as big as footballs.

In all, the city was a ghost town, and it was an eerie feeling. Most if not all citizens had been evacuated, and we were told that if we encountered anyone, then they were not supposed to be there. More on that later.

On arriving at the ATF *ad hoc* command post, Darian and I soon met all the agents who had arrived from around the country. Most were new agents who had obviously been drafted against their will, but all knew the historical importance of why we were there. It reminded me of the Los Angeles Riots to some extent. All of us were split up into squads, and I became leader of my unit. By leader, I mean I had to answer to the brass – people I'd known for many years; I gave no orders – we were all in an unknown war zone and each had an equal say.

Our first briefing was cool. There were a couple special agents in charge (SACs) present who explained to us what our duties would entail. Basically, we were to patrol the streets at night and make sure no shit hit the fan. As stated above, any citizen on the streets of New Orleans after dark (or at any time in certain wards) was not supposed to be there; it was our job to confront these individuals. Having worked Los Angeles I was ready for any challenge: I had a .223 caliber rifle as well as other weapons. Yet, I couldn't help thinking of *Black Hawk Dawn* and what those guys went through. Thank God, it was nothing like Mogadishu. The SACs also explained to us that all standard operating procedure was out the window.

Usually to perform any enforcement operation, you had to prepare a twenty-page operational plan detailing everything from personnel involved, criminal information, communications, nearby hospitals, shooting policies (a cover-your-ass addendum) – all kinds of stuff. The SACs told us that op plans were out, and we were told to do what had to be done. What that meant no one really knew, but basically there was a tacit understanding that if you had to shoot someone, then do it. Of course, that was okay with me.

Lodging was another story. Luckily, each of us was able to get a room in a downtown hotel. The city was deserted mostly, and all the hotels were severely damaged by flying debris or had other problems. Our particular hotel had running water (though we couldn't drink it) and there was no maid service. Big deal. I had packed for the long haul. I did have a bed, and that was nice – I wasn't even expecting that. Food was taken care of for us by some local agencies and goodwill organizations. We ate well, better than we probably deserved, and I made it paramount that I let these people know how thankful I was. They were angels.

The first several nights of patrolling the streets were tense to say the least. No one knew what to expect, so we were ready to shoot it out if need be. There had been scattered reports of lootings, gunfire, as well as citizens shooting at helicopters in the days prior to our arrival, so we took nothing for granted. Yet, all we found were deserted streets, trash everywhere, utter destruction. It made me cry.

I had been to New Orleans twice in the past, and each time had left a bad taste in my mouth. Each instance I had gone there with a significant other whereupon we had fought, and I had packed my bags and headed to the airport alone to get the fuck out of Dodge. This trip, however, would instill New Orleans in my psyche as the Emerald City of Oz. And, not because of what I was seeing, but rather what I knew the future would bring. Walking and driving those stinky streets all those nights left one thing tattooed on my brain: this city would rise again, and would elevate itself higher than it had ever been. I just knew.

That dream came to fruition in February 2010 when the New Orleans Saints won the Super Bowl. For anyone who doesn't believe or has doubts in a Higher Power, just rewind the past five years and see the strides that area has taken.

As stated, the first nights were stressful, but as days turned into weeks, we soon realized that no one was around. The only denizens left walking the streets were dogs and cats that the owners had left behind. This was doubly sad. We would soon become the Pet Police, for we hooked up with many SPCA and Humane Society-type folks who were also in New Orleans to save these deserted creatures. I'm happy to say we had a hand in helping many neglected pets find new homes all over the country. Many even came to Phoenix, I found out later.

We did have a few run-in's with assholes however. Nothing reached LA Riots stages, but we did have a few encounters with some idiots who were out for some souvenirs. We quickly took care of them and were on our way. We also recovered several firearms and other contraband, but instead of dealing with paperwork we just threw the items in the Mississippi River. No one was going to find that shit unless he had a key to Davy Jones' Locker. We, along with the United States Marshal's Service and the New Orleans Police Department, shared the streets at night, and we developed a great working relationship.

Lots has been written about the New Orleans PD and all the corruption that followed Katrina in its wake. We saw none of this. The NOPD gave us carte blanche and saw to our every need; it couldn't have been more supportive. Like most big-time departments, a few bad apples can besmirch the agency's reputation for years if not decades. Again, it reminded me of Los Angeles, but like LAPD, these officers were nothing but professionals.

After a week or two, several ATF squads were sent to Lake Charles, Louisiana, to help out in the western part of the state; Hurricane Rita had wreaked havoc there and we would have similar such duties as we had in New Orleans. On arriving in Lake Charles, we bore witness to even more sadness and devastation. Though less populated than the New Orleans metropolitan area, western Louisiana was in shambles. Beach homes had been completely lifted off their foundations and deposited wherever Mother Nature saw fit. Huge ocean-going vessels littered city streets in their own kind of rush-hour traffic jam. Dead fish, cattle, critters, everything not nailed down (and even that which had been nailed down) littered the countryside. I didn't get to see the devastation from the air, but it must have looked like the Intracoastal Waterway had pursued a new course and laid waste to everything in its path. It reminded me of pictures of the Upper Nile in Egypt and the Sudan after torrential flooding. It was gut-wrenching.

There wasn't a lot for us to do in Lake Charles, so we would find things to do. Every late afternoon we would go on "gator patrol." This entailed driving south down in the vicinity of Grand Lake and looking for alligators. We found several, but most were just little dudes. Their species had survived everything from the Ice Age to the great floods, so the hurricanes must have meant little excitement to them. Unfortunately for the civilian residents, the destruction was cataclysmic.

After a week or so we returned to New Orleans. My squad then resumed its old duties. Darian and I had taken a detour on returning to New Orleans. We had journeyed to Avery Island, just south of Lafayette, Louisiana, which is the home of Tabasco Hot Sauce. Darian was a Tabasco fanatic, so I had to go along, and I'm glad I did. You could smell the place five miles away – a heavenly scent if you liked the stuff. The place was pretty much shut down, but Darian and I made some hefty purchases at the gift store: him because he loved Tabasco; me, because I tried my best to pump any money back into the local economy.

The only new intelligence we learned on returning to New Orleans was that it was now okay to drink the tap water, but none of us took any chances. So, we resumed our nightly ventures, which as stated above, became more pet rescue than a police mission. That was fine with me; if I could help in any way, I was glad. And, so were the locals.

Our nights became shorter, and we soon began arriving back to the hotel at earlier hours. Since there was no television or night life (the French Quarter would partially reopen near the end of our stay, but most of us stayed away), I needed to find something to do.

During my past – all the way back to my high school years – I had picked up the hobby of writing short stories. I had never had any published (never tried), but the pen became my solace for dealing with many bad or unexplained phenomena in my life. I could never just sit down and force myself to write; rather, inspiration and thematic content just came to me over the years whereupon I would be at the mercy of the pen. Such an episode happened in New Orleans during those latter days. To this day I can't explain it.

Most of my fiction was very Steinbeckian, that is, after reading the reader was usually left with a strange taste in his mouth. Though some themes were shocking, the overall purpose of my writing was to make the reader think. Yet, the story I would compose in New Orleans became something I have not been able to explain to this day. I was surrounded each day and night by death, destruction, sadness, hopelessness, and fear. Yet, the story I pumped out in that hotel room was a love story – something entirely 180 degrees from what I was seeing in my nightly travels. My writing was not known for very many happy endings, but this work of fiction became my favorite story of all.

After five or six weeks, our time in New Orleans came to an end. We hadn't done a lot, but the townsfolk let it be known how appreciative they were that we had come. I didn't ask for any pats on the back, but I did feel proud that someone had taken notice. I knew Louisiana was years away from any type of return to normal everyday life, but I was happy that I may have played a part in that city's rebuilding. I knew God would see to that, and in time He did just that, though it is still a work in progress.

My thoughts and prayers to everyone who had to endure Nature's wrath, but like Ernest Hemingway said, "Man can be defeated but never destroyed."

Chapter XXIX

Training Day

Since I had been a professional athlete before ATF, I developed a training regimen that would carry me through my entire career as a federal agent, though there would be some variations. I put this chapter near the end of the book because readers tend to remember what they read last. And, over the years, too many federal agents have lost sight of their bodies. What that meant was they also lost sight of staying in real shape.

Everyone should take their job seriously (but not *too* seriously), and in terms of staying in shape, I always wanted to be at the top of my game. I always wanted to be able to kick the criminal's ass if it came to that, and I didn't care how big the guy was. It wasn't a narcissistic thing; it was a survival thing. Thanks Dad.

ATF preached this ethos in the beginning and at its Academy, but somewhere down the line it lost track of putting fit agents on the streets. We had men and woman as agents that probably hadn't seen their feet in years and would probably have had trouble taking a piss. That's not good. I don't want that person on my search warrant. ATF had no follow-up physical conditioning tests or requirements over your career (as it stringently does in, say, firearms), or similar ways to measure that its agents were truly working out for those paid four hours per week. Four hours wasn't enough for me, but it is enough for most people. The following regimen was my own, but rest assured there are many *old school* ATF agents who took this shit as seriously as I. Their regimens were equally as diverse and grueling. That's why we were the *best* agents – and take notice, I said *were*.

At the Academy I won the Eddie Benitez Physical Fitness Award, which is awarded to the agent who scores highest on a series of physical tests. I didn't get a perfect score – guys like my boy Brad Brown could pull that off – *AND*, after partying for all hours the night before! – but I did win the award. I was proud as shit for that honor. I knew Los Angeles: I knew if it ever came down to hand to hand combat (thank God, it never did), I would at least have a dog in that fight. I'm not a big guy, but I was strong. That's all I needed, and I maintained a desirable level of strength my entire career.

Los Angeles training was about as diverse as you can get. I ran, swam in the ocean, surfed, biked, lifted weights, and hiked the Santa Monica Mountains like it was going out of style. When I first got hired I had my weights in storage in Ventura, California. I would wake up and go to the storage complex – pull out the weights, do a workout, not even shower, and get my ass to work. That was fucking dedication, I do say. I even procured weights from the place where we used to burn our evidence, a huge foundry in Southgate, California. The people there were always great to me, and gave me great deals on weight training equipment that the foundry commercially produced. I have much of that same equipment today.

Hiking was another story. Since hiking burned a lot of time, my friends and I trained at night. Night hikes in the Santa Monica Mountains became legendary and were invented by a close friend of mine named Ronald Wolf*. I grew up with Ron and his brother (they lived in Pacific Palisades, which is the next contiguous town from Malibu to the south). They and their angelic mother had let me crash at their house over the years when the Pacific Coast Highway was closed (due to mudslides) or if things weren't going so well for me at home. Ron got me into hiking feverously; I'm talking *psychotic* hiking! It wasn't your normal Yellowstone path up to Ol' Faithful.

It would begin with supplies: beer, food, ammunition, and extra clothing. Ron wasn't into our shenanigans, but he knew the trails, so he had to come along. He was our Sacagawea. Tunes were the next essential. In order to keep critters away (and *people* for that matter), we would bring the most obnoxious and offensive music we could gather (i.e., offensive to other people): the Meatmen, Slayer, punk rock, you name it. We even recorded our own music. It would scare the shit out of any animals, but it would truly scare the shit out of some kook who happened to be hiding in the hills from the law. Don't laugh, this happened several times. There were several nights when police helicopters were lighting up the hills looking for somebody. Some of my hiking mates used to be very paranoid at times – thinking that the cops were after us because we were shooting guns in the hills, but we never got lit up by a chopper. But, we didn't take any chances either.

I would even take an ATF radio with me on occasion on these excursions. I would talk to whoever the duty agent was that night. You know, run a license plate in the sky. Night hiking became the ultimate cardio endeavor. You could party all night long, get a great workout, and burn all off by the time you got to the end of the hike – which was anywhere from four to nine hours later. It was flawless! I was in it for the camaraderie and the sweat, but some of the crews that ventured into the hills were on other planets. You name it, they were on it, but I would not stand for any slackers. You could do whatever substance you wanted, but you weren't going to bring me down (thanx, Mike Muir!) or keep me from getting my workout in. All I know is I got into the best shape I had ever been in my life, and that includes high school football, basketball, anything. And, it was fun.

One particular night hike is worth relating. For some reason we decided on a new route; our usual hike was called "The Loop," and was about an 13-mile excursion from Pacific Palisades and the beach to the San Fernando Valley and back. This particular evening we decided to do The Loop backwards, or as we called it, "The Pool." I had to assist a search warrant the next morning, so we got an early start so I could eventually get some sleep. Somewhere along the trail I misplaced my Smith & Wesson Model 66 revolver. I always kept it tucked in front of my pants in a holster, so in order to urinate (a frequent occurrence) I would remove the gun and holster. Apparently, I had forgotten to put it back. Well, the hike went very long that night – you could never gauge how long you'd be out there. Sometimes we'd finish in record time; other times we wouldn't finish at all. About three quarters into the hike I realized that I had lost my gun. My ATF gun! I left my partners and retraced the entire hike. I eventually found the firearm resting on the trail many miles back, but by the time the night was over, I had been on the trail for nearly eleven hours! I quickly hiked down the hill to my car and drove directly to the search warrant. I definitely wasn't at the top of my game during that enforcement activity, but I made it there nonetheless. That was a long night!

Since I was an ATF agent, I had access to lots of cool gear. This blends into more of my Colorado days, but I would travel back to California on occasion for pre-scheduled night hikes. In Denver, a buddy of mine had a hook with the military where we would procure army surplus stuff for free. I took huge advantage of this. I must have procured dozens of mummy bags, backpacks, canteens, entrenching tools, bug nets, camouflage clothing, you name it – for me *and* my bro's. You see, night hiking took a toll on your textiles. I went through BDU pants like underwear. So, my army connection was huge! Plus, we looked like freaks should we encounter anyone on the trail. We would dress up in full flight suits, with bug nets, camouflage. If we had ever encountered anyone, they would have thought the Santa Monica Mountains were being invaded.

I would bring my sidearm with me on all hikes – for protection and for fun – and usually several hours into the hike, we'd all stop and shoot off some rounds. We were well out of earshot of civilization, though I'm sure we scared the shit out of any inquisitive wildlife. I've always been a gun safety freak, and all shoots were conducted safely and without incident. Some of you may be asking how anyone drinking or on drugs could possibly be safe with a firearm? Sometimes being mentally challenged causes one to concentrate even more. You wouldn't know this because your teetotaling deportment can only allow you to pass judgment without experience. Remember, I never said we were angels, but that's according to *your* yardstick, not mine. Enough said.

Hiking became the chief love of my life; I lived for it, and this I would transplant to Colorado upon my transfer. However, the Rocky Mountains brought hiking to a whole new level. This was the Major Leagues. I became a mountaineer. Colorado is famous for having fifty-four (54) fourteeneers, or 14-thousand foot peaks. Curiously, it doesn't have the highest fourteener in the lower forty-eight states; that esteemed recognition goes to Mt. Whitney in California. Nonetheless, Colorado was a mountaineer's mecca, and I made it my own.

Every weekend from late spring to late summer I would drive all over the state and attempt to climb fourteeners. I say *attempt*, because there were many times when the elements or chance had other ideas. In all, I climbed over thirty of them, some of which were just walk-ups, others that I nearly lost my life on. The rush and workout were inexplicable. And, the beauty: unrivaled. I can tell a story about each peak and even recognize them all from 35,000 feet. Those memories I'll cherish forever.

I also became a huge snow rat. Growing up on the beach, you would think that winter sports would turn me off. Far from it. Besides snowboarding, I became the snow-shoe guy from hell. This became my favorite winter training mode, and you talk about a hell of a workout. Just imagine being on a stair-master for two hours but being surrounded by ponderosa pines, deer, elk, snow bunnies (the four-legged variety), everything. It was paradise, and a grueling workout.

I also got into rope-less rock climbing in Boulder, Colorado. This was particularly dangerous, but it caused me to block everything out and just climb. I would do anything to challenge and hone my concentration skills. I did have a few close calls though.

I also loved doing sprints – especially in the snow. I would go to a local park and take a football along with me. The routine was I'd punt the football as far as I could, and then I would sprint to where it stopped rolling. I would do this for an hour or so, or until the football ran out of air (which was common when the temperature was below freezing).

In Phoenix I continued my hiking ways. Many don't know this (or don't bother to notice), but Phoenix is surrounded by beautiful mountains, valleys, and picturesque hikes. Some peaks just northeast of town tower above 7000 feet. These places became my new homes. The Superstition Mountains – of Lost Dutchman's Mine fame – sat 30 miles due east of Phoenix in the town of Apache Junction, and this became my weekend haven for working out. And, the hikes were grueling – especially in the summer time. I would also hike Camelback Mountain, a popular 1 ½ hour hike in Scottsdale. This hike was usually very crowded, but I would bushwack my way to other parts of the park where I wouldn't have to deal with any people.

Rattlesnakes were another matter. Since I always had a walk-man or IPod on, I nearly stepped on many pit vipers who were only sunning themselves in the afternoon. No disasters, thank God, though I did come close on several occasions.

Physical fitness meant everything to me, and even before I became a federal agent. Nonetheless, I knew it was important for my job as well, and I took great pride in trying to be in the best shape possible should I need to be. ATF talked a good game about physical fitness, but in all it was afraid of forcing any agent to do anything in the belief that it would be sued or grieved at a later date. Pretty sad, especially considering how important ATF made you think physical fitness was in the beginning at the Academy.

Again, just another lie.

Chapter XXX

Final Days

The following chapter is going to be emotionally and mentally tough for me to recount, but it has to be related because this will probably be the only chapter my enemies, notably ATF, care to remember. It is a chapter of my life that is ongoing and one of struggle. Yet, belief in myself – not belief from ATF or any other detractors – has been what's paramount. I apologize to the reader for jumping around in the pages that follow.

And one note: I am not a lone case study; ATF has fucked over many an employee and will continue to do so.

My life really began circling the drain in the middle of 2004, though many factors leading up to it go back much farther. In May/June 2004 I was diagnosed with extreme pneumonia and was hospitalized for two weeks. I was later told that I nearly died – though no one needed to tell me because I felt like I was dying for three months. What brought on the pneumonia was a somewhat minor sinus infection that subsequently settled in my right lung. Initial treatment involved draining both lungs of the fluid, but a full-blown operation ensued in order to save the right lung. This procedure involved entering my body from the backside, breaking three ribs, and then venturing into the lung to clean out the gunk that was described to me by the surgeon as looking like rotting seaweed. I subsequently burned fourteen years of sick leave and missed three whole months of work.

My sinus problems go back to birth, and over the years I had tried just about every treatment on earth: prescription drugs, over-the-counter stuff, holistic treatments – you name it. After a while I just decided to live with the irritation and the chronic cough that came with it.

There's an amusing story when my father took me to a pulmonary specialist while I was in college. The doctor asked me how long I had had my terrible cough, and I nonchalantly replied, "Oh I don't know, probably ten years." Though I didn't really see the immediate humor, the reply got a good laugh out of everyone present.

Over the years the cough had gotten considerably worse, though I still just decided to live with it. The mountain air of Colorado did lessen the symptoms somewhat, but it was my transfer to Phoenix that things got really bad.

Many people move to the desert because of the clean air, but I can assure you that Phoenix has some of the driest, dustiest, and most polluted air in the western United States, especially in the wintertime.

In the late spring of 2004, the shit hit the fan.

What no one knew at this point was that I had become an abuser of over-the-counter medicines – everything from cold pills, cough medicine, to just about everything in the cough-cold aisle. By May 2004 my body had obviously had enough, and I paid for it dearly. I lost over 20 pounds, including years of muscle mass that I had built up since college.

After the operation I obviously was set up with all sorts of good "medicine," and this was prescription hard stuff. The pain was excruciating, and after the prescriptions ran out, I returned to the over-the-counter stuff to kill the pain. Alcohol also became a huge problem. I had always been a big drinker, but I had never let it interfere with my occupation. Alcohol also became my way of masking my intake of everything else going into my body. Though I never drank on the job, I usually couldn't wait to get home to start up again; and, since I was now in administration and working normal business hours, I didn't have to worry about waking up at 5 A.M. to go on a search warrant or other enforcement operation.

Things only got worse, for in the fall of 2004 another tragedy occurred in my life. My mother, who lived in southern Florida, had her residence destroyed by two hurricanes that year that had chosen to make landfall in the town she lived. When the second hurricane hit, I was in Newark testifying in a case. I had to change my travel plans in order to get her out of Florida. I subsequently flew to Florida, rented a moving van (one of the last available in the state), and moved her and all of her belongings to Phoenix. We loaded up my mother's car with every breakable item, and made the 2000+ mile drive back to Arizona.

It was traumatic for everyone involved, but exponentially draining on my seventy year-old mother. She died in January 2005.

God was on both our sides, however, for my mother's only wishes were to see the Boston Red Sox win the World Series (which they did in

2004) and to be with her only son as she lay dying. Neither one of us foresaw that she would die after only four months after arriving in Arizona. After her death, I really began hitting the booze and over-the-counter stuff hard. She had been my best friend in life, and anyone who has ever lost that person knows what that entails. I don't use this circumstance as an excuse, only as a catalyst for what would happen in July 2006.

By that time I had been transferred to the Arson & Explosive Group, but my problems continued to spiral out of control. In July 2006 I was arrested for DUI and subsequently convicted for the offense. I would pay in upwards of $6000 for the ordeal, and my career was now under intense scrutiny, and rightfully so.

Knowing how bad my problems had become, the first thing I did after the arrest was check myself into rehabilitation. I did this on my own, for only I knew the full extent of the problem, but doing so would be used against me by ATF at a later date. I had no sick leave left on the books, so I had to take a 240-hour advance as well as burn much annual, or vacation time. I didn't care, for I knew I had to put myself first. I completed the program and actually felt like a new human being upon returning to work in the latter part of 2006.

As I learned soon after, ATF didn't give a fuck.

Every five years federal employees have to undergo a follow-up background investigation documenting the previous five years. As a Special Agent, I had to undergo the intensive investigation in order to maintain my Top Secret Security Clearance. In my application I came totally clean about my rehabilitation as well as all the circumstances surrounding it (ATF knew everything about the arrest). As I would find out later, ATF gave two shits about the DUI (I only received a Letter of Reprimand for the episode); it was the rehab that it was truly interested in, for ATF would use all the medical records of my rehab against me. I granted the investigators full access to my medical records, and had I known in advance how that was going to put my career in jeopardy, I probably would have fudged in this area.

But, I had nothing to hide; I never did.

After some time, I was told by my SAC that my Top Secret Security Clearance was being held up because of what was in those medical records. This was in March of 2009 – nearly two and a half years after my rehabilitation. As I would find out, this was ATF's final powerplay to get me fired, for it would not only cite the DUI and rehabilitation, but ATF would also document that I had been a problem employee since the early 1990s. I had been suspended four times over the years for a myriad of offenses – ranging from embarrassing the Bureau, the Kentucky incident, my "battle" with the United States Attorney's Office in Los Angeles, to also having a firearm stolen in November 2002. All of those instances would be used by ATF to build a historical case against me labeling me a threat to national security. The irony of the stolen gun episode deserves discussion.

Sometime in the late summer or early fall of 2002, my backup revolver was stolen from my apartment. I couldn't exactly pinpoint the exact date of the theft because I kept this firearm under my mattress at home and only carried it irregularly. No one could prove who had actually stolen the gun, though I suspected the maintenance personnel at my apartment complex. I would receive a three-day suspension for the theft. The real tragedy was that an eighteen year-old boy committed suicide nearly two years later with the weapon in August 2004 in Chandler, Arizona. It should be noted that by the time of the death, the revolver had probably changed hands a dozen times; that is, the teenager had nothing to do with the theft.

The fact that the murder weapon had been an ATF firearm never surfaced, at least not to the family of the slain boy. I was subsequently returned the gun (after an in-house inspection as to its usability – catch the irony here!), and I carried it for the rest of my career.

The real irony is that I never let the ATF-nexus be known – at least not publicly; you see, I didn't want any unnecessary or besmirching press coverage to result because of the unfortunate incident. There were many days and nights that I wanted to reach out to the boy's family and express my deepest regrets for what had transpired. I knew it couldn't bring the teenager back to his loved ones, but I still had to live with this on my conscience for many years. I still do. I just took my three-day suspension on the chin (as I did with all my other suspensions) and kept my mouth shut – only because I loved the Bureau that much. I knew any press would be detrimental to ATF, so I just went about my job. Funny how things turn out. Perhaps now that I'm no longer an ATF employee I can finally contact the parents and tell them everything. Nevertheless, ATF would use this "failure to secure government property" against me in the security clearance proceedings.

In March 2009, when ATF made its full-court press to finally get rid of me based on the security clearance issue, I in turn hired an attorney – the Chief Counsel of the Federal Law Enforcement Officers

Association, or FLEOA. I had been a member of FLEOA for many years, and the latter entity had its foundations in protecting federal agents from being fucked over by its employers. Little did I know that FLEOA was all part of the same team with the employers. I would get minimal representation, and when a final determination was rendered by the Department of Justice in April 2010, my appeal for reinstatement of my security clearance was ultimately denied.

I was given the chance to retire, and I did so on April 20, 2010, exactly eleven years to the day of the Columbine massacre. Irony or poetic justice? You decide.

Two other incidents would come into play in ATF finally getting rid of me. First, in October 2007 I had another firearm stolen – this time out of my government car as I stopped for groceries one night after work. Though I wasn't in the store longer than two minutes, I had failed to secure the gun in my trunk (ATF policy), and as a result the weapon had been stolen along with my briefcase (where I kept the firearm) out of the back seat of my government car. Stolen were all kinds of personal effects: checkbooks, secondary badge, identification media, address books, you name it. It was complete negligence (or haste) on my part, and I would sustain a 10-day suspension for the theft (curiously reduced from the initial 14 days). Again, I served the suspension as I had all the others, especially since I was to blame for this particular theft, at least in terms of ATF policy.

Yet, ATF would also use this instance to bolster its case to have me fired, specifically my inability to safeguard government equipment. ATF's reasoning was that if I couldn't secure a gun, then I couldn't possibly safeguard national security information. My peers around the country knew this was bullshit, but the bean counters in Headquarters had another agenda. The argument against me was weak at best, especially since no one loved (or loves) his country more than I. Yet, ATF and the Department of Justice (the ultimate deciding entity) didn't see it that way. I'm not the only one in history who has been singled out and denied a security clearance for opaque reasons. Remember J. Robert Oppenheimer in the 1950's and that travesty of "justice."

The other incident used against me was another arrest I sustained in July 2009. I was subsequently booked for Drunk in Public as well as urinating in an alley. The latter charge was true (I was caught in the act), but the former is comical and entirely false because I was actually escorting a drunken friend to his residence one afternoon because *he* was intoxicated. I had even chosen to walk him home down an alley to be discreet.

Four to five police cruisers soon descended upon the alley, and the only reason I was arrested was because the first responding officer, a female, panicked (why, I have no idea; she even threatened to taser me as I asked her for assistance with my friend), and also because I vociferously made it known to all soon-to-be-responding officers that I was tired of all the harassment I had received from them for over five years.

My history with this agency, the Scottsdale (AZ) Police Department, went back many years and other than loud music mostly stemmed from an incident where police officers had come to my home after a roommate had suffered a seizure and cut open his head quite severely. The paramedics had come to my house, but for some reason the police decided to piggy-back the call and have an agenda all its own.

I invited the officers inside my home, but once inside it became quite clear that the cops gave two shits about my bleeding friend. All they cared about was my book collection in my living room, especially many books I had on German history. If they had looked harder they would have found a variety of subject material (I own over 400 books) – everything from nuclear physics to Gothic architecture.

What ensued later is even more ridiculous. I learned several days afterward that the responding police officers had been querying every license plate at my house. I found this out because I was "car guy" in the Phoenix Field Division, and any time an ATF tag was computer queried by any police department, I was the point of contact with the Arizona Motor Vehicle Division and would be notified.

I thought nothing of it at the time, but a week after the paramedic episode I found out that certain Scottsdale officers were *still* running my license plates. Now I knew something was up.

I even was told who the particular officers were that were conducting the queries, but when I tried to contact them I was never called back. Now I was getting pissed off, but the pièce de résistance occurred soon after when I received a tip from a friend within the Scottsdale PD that the latter department had begun compiling a dossier on me and my possible white supremist leanings! True, I possess books about Nazi Germany (I studied much history in college and high school), but like I said above, had they looked harder they would have realized that I also have an extensive collection of books about Russia, France, global exploration, Middle Eastern history, as well as the classics. However, these "police officers" didn't care about that. Even though they knew I was a federal agent, they still had their suspicions that I was a white supremist.

As soon as I received this intelligence (or *lack of* on the part of Scottsdale PD), I went to the SAC and told him that if he didn't take care of all this crap, then I would take care of it myself. My boss in turn met with the Scottsdale PD Chief that very day who put an end to the whole "misunderstanding."

Or so I thought. ATF would use these sets of circumstances in its ultimate play to get rid of me for good, citing my continued historical tendency to get into trouble and besmirch the proud name of the Bureau.

Another more important and tragic factor came into play in early April 2010. On April 5, 2010, my best friend in ATF murdered his wife and then took his own life in a double homicide. I had seen him only a few days before the killing, and there had been no signs that things had gone terribly awry in his life. The real tragedy was that five children were left without a mother and/or father. Though I didn't know the wife's children, I was very close with my friend's son and daughter whom he had from a previous marriage. Over the years they had come to my house, swam in my pool, and played golf with me. The real pain came from knowing that all the kids would have to live with this black cloud for the rest of their lives.

As I would find out later, ATF gave two shits about this or any collateral damage affecting others drawn into this maelstrom, myself included.

On hearing the fateful news, I couldn't believe it. I knew my friend had been doing extensive undercover work against a host of criminals, and I thought for sure the killing had been a hit. Moreover, on the night of the killing, a local cop in the area had also committed suicide. Since all the killings had taken place in a small town – not in Phoenix – I was doubly sure it was a contract hit. I never did find out what happened to all three victims, but as quickly as the incident hit the news, the incident was filed away forever. As stated throughout this book, this event wasn't the first time an agent friend of mine had died questionably or tragically, but like all similar sad incidents that occurred to ATF agents, ATF was only happy to make sure the story disappeared as quickly as possible.

And disappear it surely did.

But, not from my mind. As a result I began to abuse substances again. For some reason, after the double homicide I became surrounded by ATF Peer Support people. Apparently, it was believed by someone in ATF that I was the next person to go ballistic, especially since the dead agent and I had been great friends and because of all the personal shit I was going through with my security clearance.

I must say that the Peer Support people were great, but in the back of my mind I could never dispel the thought that perhaps ATF was only making this play toward my "well-being" because it was covering its own ass. For example, had I gone on a subsequent killing spree (something I would never do), ATF would be able to tell the world that it had done everything in its power to see that I didn't lose my sanity. Granted, my sanity was stretched pretty thin, but I never have had the balls (or incoherence) to take it to the level of seemingly senseless violence. Either way, ATF was covered.

I'll let God make the final judgment here.

Since 2006 I have enrolled in rehabilitation four times – not because of ATF (though I was urged to by many superiors), but only for myself. As a result, I have begun to clean up my life though I do fall off the boat occasionally – all addicts do. Yet, the real kicker came after I had quit ATF, and this deserves discussion as well. Another sad fact about your federal government.

After resigning from ATF on April 20, 2010, I was approached by numerous administrative personnel in order to finalize any and all paperwork with the agency. I was also approached with a proposition. I was told that I should look into applying for a Disability Retirement (DR) from ATF based on my alcoholism. Since alcohol had been the single biggest reason precluding me from continuing with my duties as an ATF Special Agent (viz., that I couldn't hold a security clearance required for my job title), I was told I may be entitled to a DR. I was told that all paperwork would have to be filed with the Office of Personnel Management, and that many former ATF employees had gone out on such a retirement.

At first I scoffed at the notion, especially since I had never asked for a free cent my entire life. Yet, the more I thought about it, the more I realized that maybe it was a viable option. Many in ATF stressed that I apply; I was told that I'd be netting somewhere around $50,000 a year, and tax free! Moreover, in my first year of being under a DR, I would be receiving a whopping sixty percent of the average of my three highest salaried years (or High Three as it is called), or somewhere in the neighborhood of $73,000 – also tax free. We weren't talking about peanuts here, and if anything it was a way to stick it back to ATF and the federal government for their inauspicious treatment of me.

After additional ponderance and *pre*ponderance, I realized that over my 20-year career as a federal agent I had pumped hundreds of thousands of dollars into Social Security, federal taxes, Medicare, Medicaid, and a host of other government programs. I soon began to justify that I was entitled to some of these federal monies, especially since my employer, a federal agency, had fucked me over and prematurely ended my illustrious career.

After much thought I applied for a DR in January 2011. I was instructed by ATF personnel that I would have to file a similar disability request with the Social Security Administration, which I also did.

I was eventually denied of both – which to be honest – lifted the huge onus that I was carrying.

You can be the judge here, but like I've said throughout this entire book, I'm no angel – but that's only measured by your yardstick. My Higher Power looks at me in an entirely different light.

Part Four

The
Future (?)

We take care of everyone else, not out own, - Donald Trump

Chapter XXXI

The Future of ATF: Gassed and Spurious

In the Prologue I detailed why I chose ATF as a career, and ironically in the notes that I memorized for my 1990 panel interview, I talk about how not to do anything that would get me or the Bureau in trouble, specifically in terms of morality, legality, etc. These words were indeed prescient in a number of respects, but I feel that I conformed to these self-imposed parameters. My ex-employer would of course disagree, but that's for the reader to decide.

The more pertinent question is this: has ATF done anything that could get itself in trouble in terms of morality, legality – and to put another term in there, integrity? The answer to this query is evolving daily, but looking back over the last twenty years, there were warning signs – and the majority of cases rests with faulty leadership.

My first encounter with ATF's questionable leadership started with the Los Angeles Riots of 1992 (see Chapter VII). ATF brass wanted no part of the chaos, despite the fact it could have played a major role in preventing thousands of firearms from hitting the streets. To ATF's leaders it was merely a local problem. The Bureau skated quite nicely through the aftermath of investigations, only because the Los Angeles Police Department purged itself of all its principal players and their gripes in the months that followed. It was a classic ATF Houdini act, and one that would be emulated many times in the future.

Waco was another travesty, and had not the Oklahoma City Bombing occurred in 1995, ATF may not have recovered from all the cover-up and finger-pointing. I had a personal friend kill himself over Waco, and not because of anything he had done wrong – only perhaps because he was made to think that he had. In Waco's aftermath ATF looked hard for scapegoats and found many – some who obviously couldn't handle it. Certain people, mainly upper management, should have been tried criminally, but as we all know, that rarely happens and unfortunately didn't happen in this case. They were all pensioned out and passed into historical obscurity. Thank heaven for OKBOMB, for it may have saved the agency. However, the façade of capable management did not escape the eyes of the rank and file.

The rest of the 1990s was also a joke, but luckily for ATF no media-fueled scandals took place. Yet, internally the Bureau began its implosion, and though hard-working agents continued doing their job, a structure and hierarchy was put in place that should have signaled disaster. As a product of Waco, two directorates within the Bureau, field operations (i.e., criminal enforcement) and regulatory operations, were reorganized and expanded to over eight directorates – everything from Liaison to Training to Professional Development to Science/ Information Technology . Somehow ATF viewed itself as the next NASA or flag waver of professionalism. Again, another opacity.

The only thing these new directorates did was create a smokescreen to obfuscate true operations and create exile locations (a la St. Helena or Botany Bay) to send those who happened to come under public or in-house scrutiny. It also diluted the agency by creating too many chiefs and not enough Indians. It created too many decision makers, and ironically it has gotten to the point where no one can make any decision. Or wants to.

Columbine was another shameful example of how ATF wanted no part of something bigger than it thought it could handle. ATF higher-ups were scared to death of Columbine and the negative legacy it could have on the Bureau (see Chapter XIX). Had it not been for a few agents who worked their butts off in the months that followed (and who took their own initiative), this tragedy would have gone down in history as another toothless ATF endeavor or Houdini act. Another ironic twist to this farce is that the person in charge on April 20, 1999, is now touring the country giving speaking appearances on how great ATF was (and he, no doubt) during the entire episode.

Going over to the Department of Justice (DOJ) after 9/11 also made certain things apparent. ATF suddenly found itself not such a prized entity or player as it had been at Treasury; this can be illustrated by the fact that the Bureau hasn't had an appointed Director since 2006. The agency has become like "the player to be named later" in a baseball trade: the player eventually arrives and may even have talent and expertise (which ATF does), but by the time of his arrival everyone has forgotten about him or has learned to live without him (that is, taken and honed that player's skills). Another analogy is that ATF was now the "red-headed stepchild of DOJ." ATF has given away jurisdiction for decades – though piecemeal – but it is becoming apparent in many people's eyes that maybe ATF is only duplicating what other agencies can do or *are* doing, specifically agencies within the Department of Homeland Security and DOJ.

And then in the fall of 2009 came Operation Fast and Furious. This "new" investigation, at DOJ's direction and with direct oversight from ATF upper management in Arizona, was meant to allow illicit guns (i.e., purchases made by "straw buyers" in the US) to eventually (or miraculously) make their way back to Mexico and into the hands of drug cartel leaders. As a result, more "meaty" prosecutions could then be levied against the leaders of the drug war waging out of control to the south. To say this was "shooting for the moon" was an understatement. As stated throughout this book, ATF has never had the resources to go after such "big fish," and though some ATF managers in Headquarters voiced this concern, apparently DOJ didn't want to hear it. As a result, Fast and Furious took off, or in actuality, it blew up on the launch pad.

Actually, agents like me had been conducting investigations or enforcement operations like this for decades – but not in the hopes of getting prosecutions or by letting guns "walk." Given the unrealistic goals set by the United States Attorney's Office (USAO) in terms of prosecutorial guidelines, our interdictions followed our own rules. When notified by a cooperating federal firearms licensee (FFL) about a suspect, or questionable buyer, we would merely go to the FFL, let the transaction take place (no use letting the FFL lose any money) and then "rip off" the suspect buyer(s) several blocks away from the business. We did this in Los Angeles on numerous occasions.

In California at that time, anyone could go into an FFL and purchase firearms as long as he/she had a valid California identification card or driver's license. Thanks to President Reagan's granting of amnesty to millions of illegal aliens in the 1980s, many of these "new citizens" saw a huge business opportunity of going into the firearms trafficking trade. We as street agents saw otherwise. We simply would traffic-stop the buyers away from the FFL and confiscate the purchased firearms. If any of the buyers expressed indignation, they were simply told to go ahead and fight the seizure. And of course, none of them did. We took hundreds of firearms – usually high-end weapons – from ever reaching their ultimate destination, which was usually Mexico. No one questioned our tactics and we continued this type of interdiction for many years.

This tactic was also utilized in Arizona, many years before Fast and Furious ever hit the books. I know this because I participated in it. Prosecutions were slim, but nonetheless the hardware never made the journey south or to other states. In other words, no one was killed by these confiscated weapons.

It was sometime in 2009 that this enforcement activity morphed (or metastasized) into Operation Fast and Furious. No one really seemed to care about guns crossing the border, for the end result was usually Mexicans killing Mexicans; no one in the United States law enforcement community (or on Capitol Hill) gave a shit.

That would soon change.

Historically ATF has had huge problems in bringing "major league" criminals to justice in the United States; just look at all the RICO (Racketeering Influenced Criminal Organizations) cases that have gone in the shitter over the past two decades. This isn't only ATF's fault (much blame lays at the feet of the USAO), but to think that ATF could do so in a foreign country is a pipe dream. Ask DEA how hard it is to seek extradition of some of the worst criminal figures of the last forty years – something it is always trying to do despite steadfast opposition from within and without. ATF has no experience in this arena and never has. Thus, the foundation of Operation Fast and Furious was an even bigger chimera.

Yet, in December 2010 when a US Border Patrol agent was killed and two Fast and Furious guns were recovered at the crime scene, alarm bells went off. Moreover, the killing became front page national news. As a result, upper-tiered management at both ATF and DOJ began running for cover. Two congressional committees were subsequently established to get to the bottom of how one of our own could have been killed by probably one of the Fast and Furious guns. [The actual murder weapon has not been recovered, though it is believed that a Fast and Furious gun was involved, namely because two were recovered at the scene.] Ironically, if not comically, the respective political commissions are called the Senate and House Oversight and Government Reform Committees. The federal government may have difficulties policing the world but it seemingly has no difficulty policing itself – and to the tune of millions of taxpayer dollars.

As of this writing the firestorm that has erupted on Capitol Hill has only become a finger-pointing forum. Like Watergate, it has become a "Who knew what, and when did he know it?" We as United States citizens may never know the answer to that question. More irony: it took a rank-and-file agent to finally blow the horn on the entire operation. If not for the Whistleblower Act, this individual would have been jettisoned into the next universe – or like many in charge of Operation Fast and Furious, to obscure ATF directorates. It's yet to be seen if any bigwig heads will roll in all this, but you can rest assured of one thing: the upper echelons will do everything in their power to exonerate themselves (or pension themselves out). It has become Waco all over again.

One thing is certain however, Border Patrol Agent Brian Terry can never be brought back. But the real tragedy is this: how many more agents, Americans, or Mexicans for that matter, will be killed in the future? Only the Almighty has that answer, but rest assured, it will happen.

Another question is whether or not ATF will survive this crisis, for as we have seen, ATF's track record in overcoming adversity has been quite successful for decades. This time, however, may be wishful thinking.

In this day of $ trillion debt, Congress wants to find places where it can cut back; I know a place where $ 1 billion could be whacked with the stroke of a pen, and the federal law enforcement machine would not skip a beat – that is, the abolition or merging of ATF with other federal entities. It would please both sides of the aisle: downsize government by downsizing the debt. This is not fantasy here; remember Waco and its aftermath. ATF was on the chopping block big-time. The biggest proponent of folding the agency at that time was Vice President Al Gore. Many senators and congressmen were on the boat as well. Is there anyone on Capitol Hill today willing to walk down the same path? Perhaps.

In regards to the federal government, anything is possible.

Tragically, all of this has been ATF's own undoing: by turning itself upside down and placing the weak at the top and the strong at the bottom, ATF has only let itself become a doormat. It's a sad fact. ATF used to be heralded as the "Navy Seals" of federal law enforcement; now it would be lucky to even be allowed to sit in on an operational planning session.

Hopefully Congress will not only get to the bottom of Operation Fast and Furious, but will also see how much taxpayer money has been pissed away in that project as well as countless others – many that don't even involve putting people in jail. Hopefully I opened some eyes in the latter category.

There were two additional lessons to be learned from Watergate: first, following the money was the best way to really get to the core of all wrongdoing; and second, that those who occupy the top spots on the government "team" are really not that bright. The sooner Congress realizes this and wants to truly get to the bottom of what's going on (both past *and* present), then the sooner all the truth will come out.

When I was hired in 1990 the Bureau had no problem operating, and operating *successfully*, on a $300 million budget. Now it says it can't operate optimally on a $1 billion budget. You can factor in inflation, but there still remains a question that needs to be asked: where is all the money going?

Moreover (and this is the *real* question), if ATF is a small agency (which it is), how disparate and how much worse does it get as one travels up the government ladder? Does the FBI spend so frivolously? HUD? We know Congress does. I don't have a dissertation on this subject, but it's worth putting out there for debate. I would bet that the problem is more pandemic than epidemic.

Hopefully this book has opened the reader's eyes to ATF's lack of any vision. It purports to have a mission and even annually publishes a strategy as to what its objectives are. This is all smoke and mirrors. ATF has one sole mission, that is, to be around next year and procure as much money from Congress to spend in the meantime in order to toot its own horn. Unfortunately, as projects like Operation Fast and Furious are exposed and former agents write books or file lawsuits to get the truth to the public, ATF's blaring bugle (and perhaps the federal government's) will only fall on the ears of the hard-of-hearing.

In terms of former agents who tell their story about the true ATF, none strikes closer to home than the story of Jay Dobyns, an undercover agent who gave nearly a decade of his life going after the Hell's Angels. Dobyn's book *No Angel* tells a story that is both harrowing and unbelievable: harrowing, in that his life was in danger and will continue to be so every day; and unbelievable, in that he was able to maintain his sanity. Yet lately, ATF is attacking even that. ATF and Dobyns are currently suing each other for a multitude of reasons, but the main ATF trump card (or so it thinks) is that Dobyns is a wing-nut who obviously let his undercover roles get the best of him. ATF has even accused him of trying to burn down his own house (with his wife and children inside) to prove that ATF is doing little or nothing to protect him. If that's not an insult to a Hall of Fame agent, I don't know what is. To give you a good idea of who Jay Dobyns is, look no further than what a former ATF Director had to say: "Jay, if you play your cards right, you could have my job one day." Enough said, and Dobyns isn't alone.

But today's ATF has another agenda. Several years ago (and before the fire) I was sent to Florence (AZ) Penitentiary to interview an inmate who had intelligence that Dobyns and his family's lives were in danger. I reported my findings back to the leaders of the Phoenix Field Division (the same leaders who have overseen Operation Fast and Furious) who basically threw my information in the trash, despite the fact that much of what I reported deserved follow-up investigation. The brass didn't think so (or didn't care). Though I didn't know it at the time, ATF was through with Dobyns and was preparing its case to cast him to the wolves. That strategy backfired, and Dobyns will have the last laugh when it all plays out. And to the cost of millions – more taxpayer money. Dobyns, as well, is still on the ATF payroll – as are many discontented agents that the Bureau feels it safer to keep close to the vest.

But what about the countless other agents ATF cast adrift? I'm not even including myself here because I of course had a hand in my own undoing. In terms of legality, I made the Constitution very elastic at times, but when it came to putting violent criminals behind bars, I always played by the rules of law. I did push the envelope at times, but that was merely in terms of my own safety and choice. In terms of morality, many would say I demonstrated none, but that is pure hogwash. I never had a problem when ATF said I was acting outside the scope of professionalism or procedure, but I never acted against anyone who hadn't broken the law. I remain very proud of my career, and that's something no one can take away from me.

As stated, the Prologue dealt with why I wanted to be an ATF agent. Today I wouldn't even consider the Bureau as a choice in my top 100. I'd be a greeter at WalMart before I'd knock at Uncle Sam's door. That's a sad statement. ATF has become an agency run by fools and an agency that only hires robots that are merely instructed to rat out their fellow agents and keep a low or *no* profile. Putting people in jail has become a by-product of ATF, no longer the product. And that's a shame. It used to be an elite entity, one that other law enforcement people – local, state, *and* federal – looked up to and relished working with. Those days are over, and should ATF weather the current foray of storms, its image will only be that much worse for it.

Chapter XXXII

The Drug War – A Viable Solution

This next chapter is going to piss a lot of people off – only because no one wants to see or acknowledge the true problem. Though my possible solution and its methods may seem a bit draconian, there is no doubt in my find that Machiavelli would merely label them a "pious cruelty."

Since 2006 the Republic of Mexico, our southern neighbor, has been at war. Not with a foreign country, but from within with drug cartels. In less than five years, 35,000 people have been killed in this war, but Mexican President Felipe Calderon, unlike all of his predecessors, has vowed to see the conflict to its end. This, unfortunately, cannot take place without help from the United States.

And by help, I don't mean dollars, National Guard, or construction of walls along the border. Many in the US, people in Congress especially, have turned a blind eye to the growing unrest that is just beginning to spill over into America. Many have deemed it a Mexican problem, to which kudos and applause have been levied toward President Calderon for his efforts in fighting the cartels. In reality, no one in this country wants to be politically incorrect, and by that cowardly phrase, I mean no one wants to anger the millions of Hispanic voters in this country. And should immunity be granted to the millions *illegally* in the United States, no one in Congress wants to anger these prospective voters.

Again, another huge lie.

I remember being in New Orleans for Hurricane Katrina, and many of the locals were surprised to see a new ethnic group coming to Louisiana to aid in the rebuilding effort. I was asked on numerous occasions who these people were, and I could only reply, "They are Mexicans, and be ready because they aren't leaving." It's a sad but true fact; countless refugees from Mexico have come to the US in search of a better life, but the tsunami has become unmanageable. Growing up in a border state, I saw this coming over 30 years ago. No politician bothered to stem the tide then, and no politician is willing to ebb the flow now. In other words, those people are here to stay and nothing can be done about it. However, something *can* be done about the current drug war on and south of our border.

First, marijuana needs to be legalized. This would hit the cartels hard, for marijuana is their biggest cash crop and source of illicit revenue. Legalization is already happening in some states, and it's only a matter of time until it's universal. Since the federal government is big on taxation, there is no better time to give in, legalize the shit, and tax the hell out of it. Of course this move will foster a new black market, but since that resulting economic reality will be in its infant stage, it should be manageable and enforceable. I don't see how any other drugs could be legalized, though there are many who can make an argument for the legalization of any controlled substance. That debate isn't for these pages and should be taken up elsewhere.

As to dealing with the drug cartels in Mexico, my option is not only viable, but one that would be welcomed by a host of individuals, notably President Calderon. The first order of business is to get the US Military involved – and I don't mean by stationing uniformed G.I.'s in hot spots along the long and tenuous border with Mexico. I mean a formal declaration of war needs to be declared against these criminal entities in conjunction with a wartime alliance with the Calderon government. The US has basically done the same thing in dealing with al-Qaeda overseas; so, there's no argument that can be pushed saying that the drug cartels are not a foreign country or entity and therefore a formal declaration of war cannot be ratified.

I also don't mean a half-ass military commitment either. I mean all-out war. Unlike al-Qaeda operatives in the Middle East, those involved in the Mexican drug trade are much more overt and out-in-the-open – much like Pablo Escobar and his cohorts in Colombia in the 1990s. Because of this flaunting of power and influence, we basically know *who* they are, and for the most part, *where* they are. Collateral damage, that is, the killing of civilians, would be minimal. These criminals have also no reproach when it comes to waging war: beheadings, murder of government officials, murder of judges, murder of just about anyone.

So, why should we? There's an old adage in war, that in order to be victorious you have to be one level more brutal than your opposition. This was the lesson learned in Vietnam (or what *should* have been learned); the United States was afraid to take it to that level in order to win. The enemy threw all the Geneva Conventions/Accords and war "rules" out the window, and as a result the Communists prevailed in Southeast Asia.

In war there *are* no rules, especially when your opponent completely disregards all signs of humanity. Unfortunately, this current crisis isn't about being humane; it's about getting rid of these assholes – all the way from the drug kingpins right down to the street dealers. If civilians don't want to get killed, then don't sell or traffic narcotics. A full military push by the US military in conjunction with the Mexican government could take care of this problem in a month. It would be brutal; it would be inhumane, but like I said above, the only way to victory is to be one step more lethal/brutal than your opponent. It's a sad fact, but a fact nonetheless.

Many would say that our military is stretched too thin at the current time, being that it is still concentrated in the Middle East as well as other theaters. My answer to that specious argument is a rhetorical question. Why the hell are we over there anyway? Why are we still in Korea after six decades? In terms of Afghanistan, we've already been there longer than the Soviets in the 1980s, and *they were next door* and couldn't do a damn thing. The terrain, the topography, and the Afghan culture will never be conquered. As Hemingway said, "Man can be defeated but never destroyed." It's time to cut our losses and get the hell out of there. Besides, Pakistan as an ally is about as formidable as a submarine with screen doors. Al-Qaeda is always going to be gunning for the United States; if its base isn't in Afghanistan then it surely is going to be somewhere else. It's too late to stem that tide. Many will say the best defense is a good offense, and I believe that is so in many respects. Afghanistan isn't one of them.

In terms of Iraq, President Obama is adamant on getting the troops home. He should be commended for this. Should Iraq spiral into civil war, then I'll ask another rhetorical question. What of it? What the hell do we owe them? Did the US turn that country upside-down for two decades, or was it always a den of lions?

Politicians need to reread their history books as to Arab culture. Remember in World War I when T.E. Lawrence led the Arab Revolt and subsequently laid the foundations for Arab self-rule, what ensued? Was it democracy or full representation of the people? No, it was a land grab by the most powerful Arab families and tribes, that is, as much land as the British and French would allow. Remember who the Hashemites were, as well as the Saudis. The *strong* will always prevail in this forsaken land, and it's an utter shame, but it's not for Americans to referee or dictate terms. I don't see any reason for being in the Middle East at all, with the one exception of the Suez Canal.

What about Israel, you ask? What about the oil reserves? In terms of the Israelis, as they showed in 1956, 1967, 1973, and countless times since, they can take care of themselves and aren't afraid to do so. I've had the pleasure of knowing many Israelis over the years, and they are some of the most courageous and admirable people on the face of the earth. I always made it a habit of asking these acquaintances, what they thought the American role would be should there be an all-out Arab-Israeli war, and I always got the same answer, "We [the Israelis] are the only ones who can take care of ourselves." Many Jewish people in the United States will have a problem with the latter statement, but you can rest assured of one thing: their "compatriots" back in Palestine don't believe they are truly representative of the Jewish people and the Jewish state. I tend to agree with them.

As to the oil reserves, all one hears about these days is cutting our subservience to the Arab nations and their reserves. Well, why don't we? Environmentalists want to play both sides of the debate, and politicians want to spout out only what their lobbyists tell them to. The US can support itself on its own oil reserves, and should that not be enough, there are always our oil-rich neighbors Mexico and Canada. Since petroleum is a finite resource, what better incentive to look for other energy solutions? Of course, the oil companies will have a say in all this, but how many of you are sick and tired of being fucked over by them?! A gallon of gasoline for over $4?! You can hate the Middle Eastern countries as much as you want, but it's our own multinationals and the politicians who protect them who are the true criminals.

So, what do we owe the countries of the Middle East? The answer: not a damn thing. Like I said, the only real vital and geopolitical interest in that region is the Canal, and only for the commerce of other goods. Trust me on this one, the Arab nation-states would be happy to see us leave, and if they're not, then that's too bad: continue to live in poverty and target the US with your acts of terror. There's no need to be proactive over there in terms of combating terror; if they hit US soil again, then we hit them twice as hard afterward. Remember what I said above about how to deal with the Mexican drug cartels.

Working in Phoenix opened my eyes to many things, none more important than the spillover effect this drug war is having on America. I also saw how nearly every gun being used in this war south of the border has its origins in the United States. That's a whole different debate and one I don't plan on undertaking with the gun lobby. I worked on many investigations that tried to mitigate the flow of firearms going south and I just know what I saw, and file this in your memory bank: <u>we aren't doing shit to stem the tide</u>. Gun trafficking is rampant in this country, and it's not an intra-country problem. These weapons are going south and no one is willing to successfully (if not mercilessly) do something about it.

In closing I want to say that I have a great regard for the Mexican people, and I feel for them every day. I have all my life. There's no racism or bias in my viable solution for the drug war; I'm only saying that it should be up for discussion. If the flood of narcotics was coming north from Canada, then I'd turn the continent upside down and preach the same solution. Of course I'd probably be denounced as being anti-French Canadian, or anti-British Canadian, or anti-Inuit. That argument holds about as much water as a three-ounce canteen for a trek across Death Valley, or the Empty Quarter of Saudi Arabia for that matter. In other words, it means nothing.

God bless America.

Afterword

Nothing in all of nature can be found to match the cruelty with which society treats its best men.
- Plato

I imagine there are many who read this book who didn't understand the title. The content of this book goes much deeper than an agent's memoir that documents a federal agency's "circling of the drain." It has to do with judgment. Not my judgment (for I know I am no one to judge anything or anyone), but rather society's quickness and propensity to judge everything.

I know my actions will be taken to task, and that's one purpose of this memoir. However, before casting any kind of judgment on me, ATF, or the federal government, one must truly look inside oneself. Today's world has unfortunately evolved into a society where everyone has a judgmental opinion – be it good or bad. Such judgments have led to the decline of one of the greatest nations in history, a free-fall that the United States may never recover. Due to finger-pointing and "not seeing the Emperor in his new clothes," the US (if not many nations) has become a society that could no doubt find fault with angels. Thus, the title *Where Angels Deserve to Die.*

If you as the reader got the title, I apologize. And remember, only you can change the path our country is heading.

Unfortunately – *and never forget this* – your leaders don't give a damn.

Acknowledgements

There are so many people to thank, and like a musician's first album, I'll try to name them all. First, I'd like to thank the One who has watched over me from my first breath. Without the guidance and care of that Entity, I surely would not be here today. I would also like to thank my editors/proofreaders Leigh Adams and George Jett, for without you two, these pages would make little sense to anyone outside the law enforcement community. I'd also like to thank the Coach House and all its employees. I miss you all.

John Steinbeck and Charles Dickens: you are my blood.

I'd like to thank every police officer in this country for risking his/her life for me every day. As I told everyone over the years, my job as a federal agent was a cakewalk compared to the normal police officer. I usually knew what I was getting into before it happened on the street; the beat officer is exactly the opposite. He/she usually has no idea what may be hiding around the corner. Staying alert and always donning your game face is something unrivaled, equaled only perhaps by the military. I love you all. I specifically want to thank the Los Angeles Police Department – the <u>best</u> department on the planet; the Los Angeles County Sheriff's Office; the San Fernando (CA) Police Department; the Aurora (CO) Police Department; the Denver Police Department; the Logan County (CO) Sheriff's Office – I luv ya Bob; the Cortez (CO) Police Department; the Montezuma County (CO) Sheriff's Office; the Colorado State Patrol – Schaeffer what's up dude!; the San Juan County (UT) Sheriff's Office; the Phoenix Police Department; the New Orleans Police Department; the Drug Enforcement Administration; the FBI; the US Marshal's Service. I also want to un-acknowledge the Scottsdale (AZ) Police Department: you may think you're big time, but you have a lot to learn; you're a joke. I dub thee "The Alcohol-Gestapo Police". You wouldn't last five minutes on the streets of Los Angeles – or Phoenix for that matter. Enough said, because everyone – your peers *especially* – knows I'm right.

I'd also like to thank my family and friends, whose support throughout this endeavor has been never ending.

Here's a laundry list of people I wish to thank, and in no particular order, <u>AND</u>, I'm not saying that the below-listed adhere *opinion or procedure-wise* to anything printed in the preceding pages; I'm just giving thanks because these people played a huge part in my life (*Isn't it* sad that I have to put a disclaimer on this?!): Jim Rome & Crew – You Fucks got me through countless days for a decade and a half; Jay Mohr, "Slam Man", greatest comedian alive and awesome Rome guest-host who's made me have to change many a pair of skivvies – I would love to party with ALL you guys – shit, I played baseball against Travis Rogers in college (I was an Anteater!) - Bombay Sapphires on me!; Bickley & MJ; Sam Kinison; Dice; Dangerfield; Henny; Mel Brooks; Bing Crosby; Jackie Gleason; Richard Pryor; "Dimebag" Darrell Abbott – R.I.P. my hero brutha; Ronnie James Dio, R.I.P.; Pete Steele, R.I.P. brutha; all the folks at The Well ("I Say We Trash This Fuckin' Place!"); Pebble; Queenie; Ed Reeser; JPS Brown; Wikipedia; Max Patkin; Gigi Curtis; Sorcha and everyone at The Cricket; Mark Petracca at UCI.

The Golf World: every page, every valet, every caddy, every "Food at the Turn" crew, every shoe-shiner, every waitress, every starter, every Pro Shop clerk, every garage guy, every club pro, every one of you who are on tour. You guys are borderline philosophers. That's what I took away from golf and stuffed in my wallet. All of you are nails!

Cartoonists – everyone who worked for the Fleischers (Popeye) back in the day as well as all those who worked for Warner Brothers, especially in the '30s, '40s, and 1950's; Jack Mercer and Mel Blanc; Art Clokey (Gumby).

Our Lady of Malibu: Sister Michele, Sister Bridget, and all the Sisters; Debbie Reheis, Cammie Colbert, and the Sutton girls; Trulio, Maguire, Herbst, Burt Young, and all my mates from OLM - we made it!

Football coaches, but don't forget about your own kids.

American Car Companies: From the CEO down to the last riveter!

Chick Hearn, Jim Healy, Jim Murray (R.I.P.), and Vin Scully.

The Entertainment Industry, and I'm not talking about the stars, I mean the following: all the crews, all the carpenters, every set director, every caterer, every make-up artist (yes, your craft is an art!), every animal handler, every cigarette girl, every grip (I still don't know what a grip is?!), every person who rides the bus to get to work and makes sure the set is perfect when all the stars arrive. Those are the true angels of the entertainment industry. There's a reason Clint Eastwood's at the top of my list: he takes care of his people. Period. So do I.

Every waitress, bartender, bar-back, stocker, hostess, dishwasher, cook, and restaurant/bar personnel: you make this country run. Shame on those who don't appreciate what you do.

The Mob (capital 'M'), and I mean the *Old* Mob. They cleaned their own laundry. How many innocent victims did you ever see in their melees? I bet you can count them on one hand. That's efficacy and efficiency to a T.

Actress Jennifer O'Neill, that part you played in '42 is one of the best ever – you nailed it! – just wanting to lay next to someone is priceless in life, and shamefully forgotten by so many; the Bloore Family; Whit; Laura; Jenny B; Klimoski; COBWEBB – luv U Bro!; Tennant, you taught me *how* to play shortstop, R.I.P. Brutha; Jim Pevehouse; Chuck Ice; Eli Grba; Butch Hobson; Clint Hurdle; Bob Apodaca; Brandon "Beetle" Bailey; Dave "Liddy" Liddell; Rob Hernandez; Kip Gross; Johnny Monell and everyone from the Bronx; everyone from Philly; Brad Pounders – greatest baseball name ever!; Tom Meagher – the 49'ers suck!; Brett Martin from UCI; Damon Carr; Trasshole; Brady Anderson; Batman; Cal Cain; Mike Gerakos; Daniel Dwyer – you and Hauser are the shit!; the Antonoff family; Wendy & Hugh Jass; RobRitchie; Chris Boensel; Romain; Glasscock; the Belchers; Mike Ness & Social D.; Rosebrock – anytime, anywhere, you're the one who's a disgrace to his country;

James Hetfield, Kirk Hammett, Lars Ulrich, Cliff Burton, Jason Newstad, Robert Trujillo & Metallica – You guys are BACK!

Adam Jones, Maynard James Keenan, Justin Chancellor, and Danny Carey: TOOL. My connection with you guys is indescribable. Added plus, gangbangers are scared as shit of your tunes as well! I put your music to good use.

Geddy Lee, Alex Lifeson, and Neil Peart - thank you for the intellectual stimulation and rush, and for providing the prototype for Musician Friendship and Loyalty.

Tony Iommi.

Tesco V & The Meatmen; El Duce (R.I.P.) & The Mentors; Buck Dharma; David Gilmour; Mark Knopfler; Steve Miller; Rik Emmett; Freddie Mercury (R.I.P.) & Queen; Rob Flynn & Machine Head; Max Cavalera & Sepultura – D-Lo will be avenged, my friend, I *promise*; Corrosion of Conformity; Van Halen; The Ramones; Queensryche; Def Leppard; Joey Shithead & DOA; Lee Ving & FEAR; TSOL; Dead Kennedys; Bad Religion; Edgar Froese & Tangerine Dream – listening to your music kept me in shape for many years; Les Claypool; Dave

Mustaine, Jr, & Megadeth; King Buzzo & Melvins; Mike Muir & Suicidal; Conklin; Silliman; RScott; the Rapf family; the MacLeod family; Alva; Peralta; Adams; Gerry Lopez; Mark Richards; Rabbit; Townend; JRiddle – I bought my first stick from you at NP; Dick Cia; Otis; Cornejo; Sam Anno; Cacciatore; Mayotte; Wink; Matt & Andy Lyon; Tazwell Buffington Rudd; Libby & Laura; Piper; Holly; Mayhak – Yo quiero Taco Bell!; the Marx Brothers; Godzilla; Michael Madsen; John Sjogren; Tim Doherty – you created a monster; the Layana family; the McAnany family; Chris Donnells; Billy Bean; Artie Harris; Vince Beringhele (sic.) – I looked up to you BIG TIME! because you were a tough fuck, but also a gentleman; Steve Stowell; Pat Benatar & Neil Geraldo; Running Eagle; RK; the Colonel; Pornstein; Mr. Mackenzie; Rocky George – you rock bro!; Mike Pierce; Kräck; Schooners; the Cayucos Tavern; Paul's Market, Francisco and your beautiful daughters; the hotdog guy next to the Cayucos Pier; Kellie's Coffee House; the Rim Griever; Chuck Hood, R.I.P. brother, I will see *you* in heaven; BlowCat; Itchy Buttho'; Farzad; Jen Warnke; IRON MAIDEN!; System of a Down – *obviously*; get back together!

Tom Araya, Kerry King, Jeff Hanneman, Paul Lombardo (and every drummer who could keep up with that breakneck fuckin' speed!). Your music may be the Soundtrack for Hell, but I put it to *good* use on the streets of LA and Denver.

Asolo boots; North Face; Nike kicks; Coors Beer (*Original,* of coors!) & Keystone Ice; Gatorade Fruit Punch; Champion Nutrition – best protein shakes on the planet!; REI; Bianchi; Bell Foundry; the Reardon family; the Bowdouris family; Matt Thompson from Denver – Tommy Victor, *Forever,* Bro!; the Collins brothers; Tad; the Stockstill family; McKenna, Justin, Joe and Cyndi Rodi – the best cook on the planet! (and mom); the Waco family; Rob Kite; Edwin Beckinbach; Wayne Baumbeck; "Boots" – my angelic neighbor on Princeton Ave; Glock; Smith & Wesson; everyone at Sturm Ruger in Prescott.

Every ATF staff member I ever worked with – you're the backbone of the Bureau and I love you all! One day you'll be appreciated.

Joe & Belinda Gordon; Darrell Dyer; Bob Wahl; Alex D'Atri; Tom Gerrity; Larry Cornelison, RIP Bro, I'll see you again; Lisa Atha; Gerry Petrilli; Bernie LaForrest; Gary Wurm; Richie Marianos; Forcelli; Greg Gant; Scott Thomasson; Chris Sadowski; Steve Ott; Bob Switzer; Bill Buford; Tony DeNardi – RIP my friend; Rick Cook; Hugo; Needles – you got your championship, Bro!; Baux; Yott; Langley; Tony Alphabet;

Dixie; the Price's; Don Veal; Ken Croke; John Ciccone; Jeff Russell; Eric "Beetlejuice" Stewart; Al Ruegg; Al Harden – the toughest cop I ever knew, R.I.P. brutha; Penguin; Booger; Iceman; Pineapple; Carr; Big E – both of you; Mike Dawkins; Doug Dawson; Kilnapp; Annette; Fritzy; Chuck Pratt – R.I.P. Bro; Ishmael – how the hell you pulled *subterfuge* out of your ass, I'll never know – *AND*, the 49'ers suck; Shawn, who I dubbed "God's Gift to the Ghetto"; Gonzalo; Chico; Carlos –> the ASAC's happy, brutha; Koz; Bird; JJ; Elvis; Mango; Slatz; Cricket; Hope; Nikki; Dave Conner – the best attorney I ever met; Jim Boma; Guy Till; Greg "Brutha" Rhodes; Kathy Tafoya; Joe Mackey; all the staff at the USAO in Denver; the Denver Public Defenders Office; KNAC; Corax; Tatanka; Hello Kitty Eric; Shane Fleming; Joe Walsh; Mein Fuhrer Stevo; April, Carson, the boys; JTailor; Gerry Arena; Mason Burroughs; Ed Dadisho; Barry Holden; Brad Galvan; Charlie "Mustapha" Smith; Costakis/Stivik; Joseph Granatino – you'll be in heaven my friend, I promise; Danny Campbell; Terry Stebbins; all my Academy mates!; all my mates at UCI; Tracy Hite – one of the few ATF women (or *agents*, for that matter) who has a set of balls; Jon Kaufman; Lowell Sprague; Bruce Stuckey; Harold Wacktor; Schwanz a.k.a. FiFi; Marcus; Traver; Bill Frangis, i.e., *Sheriff* Bill Frangis; all the Cheyenne and Colorado Springs boys – keep it rockin'!; Heidi; Buscher – Love you Babe; Stingin' Nettle and yo' sis – Tupac and Biggy Smalls will return!.

For all those I can't think of or forgot, I love you all. Stay safe. And, for all of you who have thanked me over the years for doing my job, <u>you</u> are the true angels, not me. Smoke dope, lick acid, and I am out!